"This is the book I've been waiting for! Around [...] how Christian nationalism has gripped their fam[...] can we do?' The answer, as Caleb Campbell reminds us, isn't war but a commitment to love, conversation, and in a word, ministry. This book not only corrects our perspective but also offers practical insights for lovingly disarming the false gospel of Christian nationalism."

Samuel L. Perry, coauthor of *Taking America Back for God* and *The Flag and The Cross*

"This urgent and gracious book is an answer to prayer for those of us heartbroken by the power of Christian nationalism over our loved ones. Now we have a resource brimming with practical wisdom to equip us to approach family and friends with the liberating gospel of Jesus."

David Swanson, pastor and author of *Rediscipling the White Church*

"Many thought leaders today both inside and outside the church are concerned about the global rise of Christian nationalism. What I love about Caleb Campbell's approach is that he recognizes Christian nationalists as neighbors who need discipleship in the way of Jesus. Caleb has taken the time to understand the movement from the inside, and he offers practical ways to engage in substantive conversation without shutting people down. If you share our concern that Christian nationalism distorts biblical principles, then this book will show you what to do about it. It's not enough to disagree. We need to engage."

Carmen Joy Imes, associate professor of Old Testament at Biola University and author of *Bearing God's Name*

"Caleb Campbell has given me back what I needed most of all—hope—to reengage in the most vital mission field of our time: the fight to save American Christianity from Christian nationalism. In calling Christians into this work, Campbell is first a pastor—one who deeply understands and clearly loves even those with whom he vehemently disagrees."

Angela Denker, author of *Red State Christians: Understanding the Voters Who Elected Donald Trump*

"This book is timely and crucial. The current decade has been defined by heightened political tensions that are increasingly framed through polarized religious communities. *Disarming Leviathan* is a valuable resource for Christians who are called to love those who have been deceived by the allure of Christian nationalism. The approach of this book to engage Christian nationalism as a mission field is a fresh approach that can give hope and direction to those who have struggled with this phenomenon."

Vince L. Bantu, assistant professor of church history and Black church at Fuller Theological Seminary, Ohene of Meachum School of Haymanot

"I have read many books on the dangers of Christian nationalism. They have a needed confrontational prophetic voice—which I believe is necessary. But I love how Campbell approaches this subject as a pastor with the heart of an evangelist. He suggests that instead of flipping tables, we offer table fellowship, engaging people from a place of relationship. His book isn't based on theory but on heartbreaking experiences with family, friends, and the church members he pastors, where he learned how to create conversations instead of confrontations. This book will provide encouragement, wisdom, and practical suggestions for all who want to see Christian nationalists return to the ways of Jesus."

Terry M. Wildman, lead translator and project manager for the *First Nations Version: An Indigenous Translation of the New Testament*

"As 'Christian nationalism' has become a buzzword in the United States, pastors and Christian leaders have responded in distinct ways: some have embraced the concept, many have tried to ignore it, and others have mocked its adherents or plotted their defeat. Caleb Campbell offers a better, more Christlike way, combining a sobering assessment of the heretical elements of American Christian nationalism with a deep love for the people who have fallen into its trappings. This gracious and well-researched book is an essential resource for pastors and others seeking to love their neighbors well."

Matthew Soerens, vice president of advocacy and policy for World Relief and coauthor of *Inalienable*

"*Disarming Leviathan* is essential reading for this time. Many of us who have been pushed to the margins of US evangelicalism have watched with horror and contempt at what has happened to a once deeply spiritual ecclesial movement now solely identified as a rabid extreme political movement. Caleb Campbell provides a necessary service for the church. He makes what was once hidden plain to see—a revelation of an insidious movement that has grown root and flourished in our midst. He accomplishes this act of prophetic revelation with thoughtfulness and grace, offering a pastoral path forward."

Soong-Chan Rah, Robert Munger Professor of Evangelism at Fuller Theological Seminary and author of *Prophetic Lament*

"When so much divides us, in both our nation and the church, Caleb Campbell helps us find a way forward as followers of Jesus. That way, unsurprisingly, is the way of love. For those looking to better understand not only Christian nationalism in America but also American Christian nationalists themselves, *Disarming Leviathan* is an excellent resource. It offers a sound approach with practical advice on how to bring the good news of Christ and his kingdom to those caught up in Christian nationalism."

Michael W. Austin, author of *American Christian Nationalism: Neither American Nor Christian*

"This book is a roadmap toward the radical generosity and love that we need to repair the relational and societal damage of our age."

Jon Ward, author of *Testimony* and *Camelot's End*

"*Disarming Leviathan* moves the conversation around Christian nationalism in the United States forward by providing constructive guidelines for how American Christians can faithfully respond to Christian nationalism's destructive influence. Campbell's pastoral heart permeates every word and provides a vivid example for how to stand for truth and love for the benefit of all—whether we reject Christian nationalism or not."

Andrew Whitehead, author of *American Idolatry: How Christian Nationalism Betrays the Gospel and Threatens the Church*

"Finally! A book that equips us to respond to Christian nationalism with hope and practical advice. This wisdom comes from an author who has not only studied the subject but who, for a time, embraced its message until a dramatic change of heart. This is the book to hand to anyone who has a friend, family member, or church member caught up in Christian nationalism."

Jemar Tisby, author of *The Color of Compromise* and *The Spirit of Justice*

"This is a book that moves beyond critique and into action, giving concerned Christians the resources they need to confront Christian nationalism in their communities. Caleb Campbell is a wise guide through challenging conversations and strained relationships. *Disarming Leviathan* is the theological and pastoral response to Christian nationalism that the church desperately needs."

Kaitlyn Schiess, author of *The Ballot and the Bible*

"This is one of the most helpful resources you can have on Christian nationalism. In his book Caleb carefully explains what Christian nationalism is and expertly reveals its major problems and idolatrous errors. He then goes one step further by equipping us to sympathetically understand the fears and concerns of those who are drawn to Christian nationalism, so that we might lovingly lead them back to the gospel of Jesus. The topic of Christian nationalism can feel complicated and frustrating; let this book give you the clarity you need and the encouragement and hope you have been looking for in this current cultural moment."

Vermon Pierre, lead pastor of Roosevelt Community Church and author of *Dearly Beloved: How God's Love for His Church Deepens Our Love for Each Other*

"I am grateful for Caleb Campbell's willingness to confront American Christian nationalism in *Disarming Leviathan: Loving Your Christian Nationalist Neighbor* as he wrestles with questions about what it means to have integrity as a follower of Jesus in the midst of incredibly fractured political divides. Campbell offers hopes and positive alternatives while confronting the false promises of Christian nationalism that stir up questions about safety, belonging, and our purpose as followers of Jesus."

Mae Elise Cannon, executive director of Churches for Middle East Peace (CMEP) and author of *Social Justice Handbook* and *Beyond Hashtag Activism*

CALEB E.
CAMPBELL

LOVING YOUR CHRISTIAN
NATIONALIST NEIGHBOR

DISARMING

LEVIATHAN

ivp

An imprint of InterVarsity Press
Downers Grove, Illinois

InterVarsity Press
P.O. Box 1400 | Downers Grove, IL 60515-1426
ivpress.com | email@ivpress.com

InterVarsity Press® is the publishing division of InterVarsity Christian Fellowship/USA®. For more information, visit intervarsity.org.

All Scripture quotations, unless otherwise indicated, are taken from The Holy Bible, New International Version®, NIV®. Copyright © 1973, 1978, 1984, 2011 by Biblica, Inc.™ Used by permission of Zondervan. All rights reserved worldwide. www.zondervan.com. The "NIV" and "New International Version" are trademarks registered in the United States Patent and Trademark Office by Biblica, Inc.™

While any stories in this book are true, some names and identifying information may have been changed to protect the privacy of individuals.

The publisher cannot verify the accuracy or functionality of website URLs used in this book beyond the date of publication.

Cover design: David Fassett
Interior design: Jeanna Wiggins
Cover images: iStock / Getty Images Plus: © NeoLeo, © photos777, © Dmitr1ch

ISBN 978-1-5140-0851-5 (print) | ISBN 978-1-5140-0852-2 (digital)

Printed in the United States of America ∞

Library of Congress Cataloging-in-Publication Data
A catalog record for this book is available from the Library of Congress.

31 30 29 28 27 26 25 24 | 13 12 11 10 9 8 7 6 5 4 3 2 1

TO LORI.

To the moon and back.

CONTENTS

THE APOCALYPSE

Division, Desperation, and a New Calling

THE YEAR 2020 WAS AN APOCALYPSE.

I don't mean the end of the world, zombies, *Walking Dead*–type apocalypse. I mean 2020 was a season of unveiling, revealing what was previously hidden underneath the surface.

Like removing carpet.

In Phoenix, Arizona, where I live, many of the homes are built on a concrete foundation. As the home ages, the foundation shifts, inevitably creating fractures in the concrete. For those who have carpeted floors, these fractures often remain unseen. As the carpet decays, a homeowner will at some point remove it, exposing the cracked foundation underneath.

Admittedly, small fractures are no big deal. They happen all the time and are normal. But if the fracture is large enough, the homeowners are presented with a difficult decision. Do they choose to put down new carpet and ignore the fracture, or do they invest the time, resources, and care required to make the foundation whole again?

This decision is made even more intense when the homeowners realize that the house they live in will crumble to the ground if the fractured foundation is put under extreme pressure. The homeowners may be caught off guard at what they unintentionally discovered beneath the familiar and comfortable surface that once covered their home's floor.

They may even begin to regret removing the carpet, thinking that if they hadn't, they wouldn't have this problem. Which, as you know, is not true. They already had the problem. They just didn't realize it. Taking up the carpet did not create the fracture; it simply revealed it. The removal was an apocalypse—making what was once hidden plain to see.

Similarly, the events of 2020 were an apocalypse. The impeachment of Donald Trump, the Covid-19 pandemic and related government responses, the killing of Ahmaud Arbery, Breonna Taylor, and George Floyd and subsequent public demonstrations, and the contentious presidential election (which culminated in an insurrection on January 6, 2021) exposed the profound depth of the fractures in our relationships. What started for many in 2015 as a general sense of concern or discontent exploded in 2020 to reveal divisions and disunity within their community.

Who among us has not experienced the impact of this in our relationships?

For years now people across the nation have been uprooting their entire lives—moving to different cities; changing employers, churches, and schools; leaving friends and family behind—all in an attempt to find communities that look, think, and vote like them.[1]

Lifelong members of churches have moved their membership to congregations they believe more closely align with their political preferences. Many churches, including the one I serve, have experienced substantial division and relational loss. Decades-old relationships have been shattered over political and cultural views that erupted in 2020.

Even closer to home, many of us have experienced significant strain within our friendships and families. Members of our family who were once characterized by their kindness, good humor, and gentleness are now frequently displaying anxiety and outrage. The stuff that comes out of their mouths, well, sounds unloving and unhinged. How can we respond in a healthy way?

Perhaps that is why you are reading this. You feel hopeless. You want to engage your loved ones, but it seems like most of the conversations end in rage, name-calling, or estrangement.

You wonder what is causing so many of our loved ones to talk, think, and act in ways that are contrary to the way of Jesus while still assuming it is the "Christian way"?

MY NEW ENEMY

For me one of the most painful revelations of 2020 was that many within the American church were not placing their ultimate hope in Jesus but were instead buying the false promises of Christian nationalism—a movement that calls Christian followers to take government power at all costs to advance their preferred way of being in the world. For a few this term (and its eponymous movement) is not new. They have seen similar nationalistic movements rise in the past. But for the vast majority of us, including me, this was a newly discovered phenomenon. While it may seem novel, this great beast of Christian nationalism—which seeks to destroy dissidents, misappropriate Scripture for its purposes, and encourage acts of aggression, racism, and hatred—has been lurking in the shadows of the American church for years, spoken of in whispers behind closed doors. All of that notably changed in 2020 when the beast reemerged from the darkness.

Scripture often attributes such currents of evil to greater forces being at work in the world. These powers are often envisioned as a serpent, beast, or dragon—or sometimes, the Leviathan, an ancient mythical sea monster that lives in the disordered abyss (Job 3:8; 41:1; Psalm 74:14; 104:26; Isaiah 27:1). To the ancients Leviathan was a vivid symbol for cosmic chaos and the evil powers that oppose the loving, orderly ways of God.[2] They recognized that humans could choose to align with this dragon-like power to the point of becoming like dragons themselves. Leviathan captures both the material and spiritual reality of present-day American Christian nationalism.

But how did so many of our loved ones fall prey to this monstrous power? How could so many Jesus followers support such fearmongering, rage-inducing, Bible-distorting, arrogant, deceitful, dehumanizing behavior?

In the recent atmosphere of political and social upheaval, many of our neighbors found comfort in the promises of American Christian nationalist leaders; they began looking to them for guidance, hope, and power. They were choosing to be shepherded not by spiritual leaders that look and act like Jesus but instead were being discipled daily (sometimes hourly) by organizations that championed Christian nationalists and by media outlets that leveraged anxiety about Covid-19, demonstrations for racial justice, and a contested presidential race to incite viewers and expand their influence. These organizations then sold American Christian nationalism as a godly solution that would protect followers' faith, family, and, of course, firearms. And a multitude of evangelicals bought what they were selling, supporting organizations that propagate this false gospel with time, energy, and money.

As a pastor of a suburban nondenominational Bible church, I felt like I had a good handle on the political leanings of my fellow evangelicals. I assumed most (but not all) would continue to endorse candidates that supported politically conservative policies. However, I was shocked to discover just how many of them were happily giving full-throated support to the ungodly leaders and organizations promoting American Christian nationalism.

To be clear, my concern was not about some vague multitude of Americans. I was concerned about *my* people. *My* community. *My* church. *My* friends.

They seemed anxious and outraged, swept up in the chaos of the moment. Seeking security and peace, they began to embody the words of false prophets who claimed to be standing for Christ (but exhibited very little of his Spirit). These people that I loved, people I had known to be kind, caring, and compassionate, were boldly repeating hateful, rage-filled statements about immigrants, public school teachers, and government health officials at the church potluck. In hindsight I see that some of these behaviors had been developing for some time, but I had failed to grasp how deep the rot went.

It was heartbreaking to see so many people that I had shared Communion with for years align with this beastly power. Their lifestyles did not bear the marks of the way of Jesus. Their words, attitudes, and behavior were often brutal, demeaning, spiteful, proud, profane, mean-spirited, xenophobic, reckless, and vile.

I wondered how these beloved Christians could give allegiance to a movement that blatantly disregards the true ways of Jesus and instead embraces the power of Leviathan. It seems to me that they, like the first humans in the Garden of Eden, had been deceived into thinking that the way of the dragon is more powerful than the way of God.

It was in this apocalyptic season that I began to ask the Lord, "What should I do?"

FROM ENEMY COMBATANT TO MISSION FIELD

When I first encountered American Christian nationalism, I viewed it as a heresy to be destroyed and those who gave themselves over to it as enemies to defeat. I thought that I could use the Bible to contradict their arguments and then they'd see that the ideas, perspectives, and methods they were promoting were contrary to the teachings of Scripture. In my mind my powerful arguments would lead them to repent and return to the ways of Jesus.

My intentions were good. My methods, not so much.

By viewing American Christian nationalists as the enemy, I was taking the posture of Leviathan: a combative approach that created more divisiveness and frustration. This was the wrong mindset, but I didn't know it yet. Then, I had a mind-renewing, life-altering experience (what the Bible calls *metanoia* or "repentance"), which changed my approach and set me on the path to writing this book.

One of my favorite questions comes from a podcast called *Make Me Smart*. In each episode they ask their guests, "What is something that you used to believe that it turned out later you were wrong about?" I love that question because it assumes that we can change our beliefs, even on deeply held convictions. The Bible calls this the "renewing of our minds." The apostle Paul, writing to the Roman church, says, "Do not be conformed to the pattern of this world, but be transformed by the *renewing of your mind*. Then you will be able to test and approve what God's will is—his good, pleasing and perfect will" (Romans 12:2, emphasis added).

I've had many mind-renewing experiences and pray for many more, by God's grace. The one that changed my trajectory came at the end of a very difficult season in my life. For much of 2020 I received numerous emails, texts, and phone calls from people I had served for years, accusing me of promoting ungodly attitudes and teachings. I was told I had adopted a Luciferian spirit of fear by advocating for online services during the early stages of the Covid-19 pandemic. I was accused of spreading divisive and demonic teachings such as critical race theory when we encouraged people to study the history of racism in the American church.[3] Some even shared that they believed I was aligning with the antichrist by not publicly calling our church to vote for their preferred presidential candidate.

This was especially painful for me because I had not intended to make enemies of the people that I served. By the time we entered the new year, I was exhausted, hurt, and frankly ready to quit my vocation as a pastor. This was the most challenging time of my life to date. But thanks to the tremendous support of our church leadership I was able to hang on. They were exceptionally encouraging and gracious to me and my family. Recognizing that I was wounded, they encouraged me to take an extended sabbatical to rest and heal.

During this time away, I spent a full day walking through various parks and reflecting on the relationships that I held dear that were now fractured. As I strolled through the beautiful landscape, different people would come to mind, and I would write their names down in a journal. At the end of the day I found my favorite bench that sits in a secluded spot overlooking a quiet stream.

As I sat, I began to count the entries. To my surprise, I counted over three hundred names.

Three hundred!

Three hundred broken relationships came to my mind in one day.

The pain in my guts was overwhelming.

Perhaps you know this pain. You may even have your own running list of broken relationships.

As I worked through the pages of this sad journal, I realized that many of these relationships fractured under the weight of disagreements relating to American Christian nationalism.

The pain in me continued to grow.

I had not set out to turn my friends into enemies, and yet the pages of my journal testified to the divisive nature of this current moment. I spent the remainder of the day grieving the collective loss of relationships that were so precious to me.

Though I continue to hold out hope that Jesus will bring reconciliation, many of these broken relationships haunt me. Standing against Christian nationalism in today's American evangelical church is costly. If you are reading this book, you probably know this already.

That day a flood of emotions washed over me. I felt betrayed, misunderstood, and angry. Really angry. And not the righteous kind of anger, either (though at the time, I thought it was). No, what I felt was rage.

In the days that followed my sabbatical I vowed to fight Christian nationalism in my community. I began to formulate a plan of attack. How could I defeat this great beast? What methods of warfare could I choose to take on this enemy? I was itching for a fight.

I started researching organizations that platform American Christian nationalist leaders and their ideas. I read everything I could get my hands on that explained or exposed nationalism in the American church.

Then I got a message from an employee of Turning Point USA (TPUSA). TPUSA is a conservative student organization that has exploded into a multi-million-dollar movement producing large rallies and conferences around the country as well as dozens of social media channels and radio programs.[4] They were reaching out to local pastors to promote their new "Biblical Citizenship" classes. They were hoping that I, a pastor, would host one of the classes and invite our church and the broader community to participate. I decided to take the meeting.

As I walked into the appointment, I was thinking about which issues I might want to argue about. I assumed my counterpart would be a rage-fueled and easily offended bully. I was wrong.

The person who entered the room was not as I imagined. She was a young woman, full of energy. She treated me with hospitality and was kind in her speech. She was, dare I say, joyful. At least more joyful than I was at the moment.

As we talked, she presented the curriculum and highlighted the set of issues it addressed. She said things that sounded strange to me, like, "Pastor Caleb, this curriculum helps people know that we need to stand up for what the Bible says about school choice," and "We need to stand for what the Bible says about our God-given right to bear arms."

Now was my opportunity to strike. We were talking about the Bible, my field of expertise. I was ready to combat these misinformed ideas. I was ready to go to war.

Then something unexpected happened that changed the course of my life.

In a candid moment, my counterpart said, "Politics is really important, but at the end of the day, I really just want to follow Jesus."

My heart melted.

In that moment the Holy Spirit did a work on me. I sensed the Spirit say, "Caleb, this person doesn't need your theological attacks. She needs to be graciously reached with the good news of the kingdom of God."

Instead of advancing my arguments, I said, "Tell me about how you met Jesus."

She responded, "Last year at a Turning Point USA event."

In front of me was a woman who genuinely wanted to follow Jesus but had been discipled into a distorted way of thinking about him, Scripture, and what it means to live the kingdom of God now.

I realized in that moment that this woman and the multitude of others influenced by American Christian nationalism were not an enemy to attack. They were a mission field to reach.

The days and weeks that followed were a time of profound reflection and recalibration for me. I dropped the posture of a warrior and began to ask God what it would look like for me to take the posture of a missionary instead, seeking not to defeat or destroy but to hospitably, lovingly, gently seek their restoration and call them back to the way of Jesus.

I set out to be a missionary to American Christian nationalists.

DIVING INTO THE CHAOTIC WATERS

With this newfound calling I dove headfirst into the chaotic waters of American Christian nationalism. Most of the missionaries I know have been called to reach cultures different from their own; they are sometimes referred to as crosscultural missionaries. They invest a lot of time, energy, and resources learning about the communities they are called to engage with. It would be similar for me. While I was acquainted with some of the elements of American Christian nationalism, I knew that I'd need to adopt the perspective of a student and learn more about my mission field.

I signed up for dozens of newsletters, chatted in discussion groups, participated in local rallies, engaged in "biblical citizenship" coaching calls on Zoom, hung out at "patriot pastors" meetings, and even attended the first annual TPUSA Faith Pastors Summit.

I examined the movement up close in the communities near me that adhere to it. I got to know the people, what they believe, what they care about (much of which I resonate with), and why they participate in events and organizations that promote American Christian nationalism.

While I have benefited greatly from work done by scholars that help to explain the phenomenon of Christian nationalism in America, it was important to me to meet the people face-to-face as much as possible. As one missionary said to me, "If you really want to see what people believe, look at their lived experience."

I wanted to listen to their voices and look in their eyes as they shared their hearts with me. American Christian nationalists are like every other mission field. They have values, rituals, taboos, and deep stories. To reach them I had to engage with those elements of their culture.

I discovered that American Christian nationalism is not monolithic. It is a movement composed of an interwoven network of various organizations, each with its own theological, cultural, and political commitments. It is composed of a variety of church traditions, including Pentecostals, Catholics, Presbyterians, and Baptists. They live in rural, suburban, and urban communities. Participants have varied degrees of involvement, ranging from sharing videos on social media to funneling financial support to purchasing weapons for what they believe is an impending uprising. Within these circles I've found true believers, new converts, violent zealots, and disaffected grifters. The one thing they all had in common is that they are not placing their ultimate faith, hope, and allegiance in Jesus and following the way of the cross. Instead, they are united in placing their trust in the power of the sword.

JOIN ME IN REACHING THIS MISSION FIELD

Many of us who recognize American Christian nationalism as incompatible with the way of Jesus are feeling deep grief at the fractures within our communities. How do we move forward? How do we heal the broken relationships with our friends and family? How do we heal the fractures within the church?

I believe that we can approach American Christian nationalists as a mission field using the two-thousand-year-old methods of Jesus and his earliest followers.

Like many modern cult leaders, those propagating American Christian nationalism strategically use biblical lingo and misrepresent Scripture in such a way that most of their followers accept their beliefs to be genuinely Christian. But at its core American Christian nationalism is a false gospel, a leader-driven movement seeking power and influence by indoctrinating its followers, preying on their fear, and leveraging their religious devotion. Those who believe it need to be reached with the true gospel, using the methods of Jesus.[5]

Each of us can take the role of a loving missionary, leading with hospitality, practicing the fruit of the spirit (Galatians 5:22-23), engaging in humbly subversive conversations, and inviting our American Christian nationalist loved ones to turn back to Jesus.

The purpose of this book is to equip you to love your American Christian nationalist neighbors by reaching them with the hope-filled message of the kingdom of God. In the following pages you will better understand American Christian nationalism, discover why people are buying into it, prepare yourself to engage them in healthy ways, and learn how to facilitate conversations that point to Jesus.

In this age of outrage it can be easy to dismiss or hate American Christian nationalists, but there is a better way. As you read this book, I invite you to prayerfully consider how to use these tools to bless your mission field and show them the love of Jesus.

Though this current season may seem hopeless, I encourage you to rest in the power of Jesus. He has risen from the grave, conquering evil and death, and he is faithful to deliver and restore all who turn to him.

Our role as missionaries to American Christian nationalists is simply to point them back to Jesus, who loves them and you very much.

BOOK ROADMAP

Once I discovered this new perspective of being a missionary to American Christian nationalists, I realized I needed to learn how to be a missionary! So I reached out to the missionaries I knew and interviewed them, asking them to share their wisdom. One missionary who had served for five decades shared three key components to missional engagement: study, set, and show.

► *Study the culture.* Invest time and energy seeking to understand their values, worldviews, beliefs, rituals, taboos, founding myths, and dreams. Examine the spiritual nature of their community, looking at religious practices, dogma, and the spiritual currents that run contrary to the gospel. Then discern how their values and convictions might fail to produce the good things that they long for. This will be the focus of chapters two through four.

► *Set the table.* Model a better way by living a life they admire and invite them to join you by leading with hospitality and cultivating a healthy relationship with your mission field, yourself, and God. This will be the focus of chapters five and six.

► *Show the inconsistencies.* Use humbly subversive questions to help them discover that their current convictions and values are inconsistent and that only the gospel of Jesus will produce the flourishing they desire. This will be the focus of chapter seven.

In the sections to follow I aim to show how you can love your American Christian nationalist neighbors by learning their culture, engaging in heart-level conversations, and guiding them toward humbly subversive conversations. All of this is done in the hope that they would have a *metanoia* experience of their own and turn back to the way of Jesus.

Before we continue, I want to give a brief caution. The road ahead will be long and difficult. American Christian nationalism will not be disarmed quickly. It will take thousands of conversations at kitchen counters, café tables, and small group gatherings. Many of the people we will encounter will exhibit dismissive, combative, or belligerent attitudes toward us. The seductive power of American Christian nationalism can consume those who give themselves over to it. The methods listed below are not guaranteed to bring about redemptive transformation. Only the living God can do that. Even now as you read, I invite you to pray that the Spirit of God will give you strength and guidance as you set out on this journey.

2

A FIGURE IN THE SHADOWS

Understanding American Christian Nationalism

Nationalism, the political lion we thought had died on the battlefields of World War II, had been resurrected, this time with religion mixed in. As churches fought battles with pastors to display the American flag on the altar in front of the cross, Christian Nationalism asserted its dominance on the national stage.

ANGELA DENKER, *RED STATE CHRISTIANS*

LIKE MANY WHO GREW UP in the American evangelical church, my first encounters with Christian missionaries were during special Sunday worship services. To my young mind they were brave, sacrificial, and somewhat mysterious men and women who left the familiarity of their homes to travel a great distance to a strange land to tell people about Jesus. They worked with indigenous communities to dig wells for clean water, translate the Bible into the local language, provide medical clinics, start schools, and introduce people to Jesus, letting them know that he loves them.

On the special occasions that missionaries would visit our church, they would share powerful stories of God's miraculous work. I found myself captivated by the pictures of their mission fields, which were vastly different from where I lived. After the service we would gather in the fellowship hall for an in-depth presentation of the ways God had been at work in their community and how those of us living stateside could help to provide for the needs we were hearing about.

In those early years I learned that missionaries were people who made it their life's work to serve a specific group of people and to share the good news of Jesus through their words and deeds. I also intuited that missionaries were some kind of superhuman Christians. Only an incredibly special person could be a missionary. Or so I thought.

Many years later I took on a pastoral role in my hometown. In the years that have followed I've had the great pleasure of getting to know many missionaries who were called to serve peoples all over the world. I discovered something that I hope they won't take as a slight—they are normal folk like you and me. The difference between us is not in their superhuman faith or gifting. The difference is in their calling. They are called to make disciples of a people different from the one they were born into. They are called to share the good news of Jesus and help people follow him in their day-to-day lives, which is what all Christians are called to do.

I make this observation not to diminish the work of missionaries but to encourage you. Crosscultural missionaries are people called to reach a specific culture, often in a faraway land. Many of us are called to be missionaries to a people group right here in the United States. Among those who need to be reached are those who profess to be Christians, but whose actions and stated beliefs are contrary to the gospel. American Christian nationalists are one of those groups, and we can be the missionaries who can reach them.

In this section of the book we will work to better understand our mission field. Like a good missionary we must first become students of the culture we intend to reach; only once we've established a groundwork of knowledge will we be equipped to connect deeply with, set the table for, and invite those we love into healthy discussion and reflection. First, we will explore the political beliefs, cultural values, and rituals of American Christian nationalists (chapter 2). Then, we will study the spiritual dynamic that empowers American Christian nationalism (chapter 3). Finally, we will examine some of the ways that American Christian nationalism fails to deliver on its promises (chapter 4).

STUDENTS OF CULTURE

One of the missionaries I met with during my preparation for this book worked around the world for decades. He had a wealth of knowledge and a powerful love for the people he ministered to. He told me that the best missionaries are those who make a lifetime commitment to learning—to be students of the cultures they intend to serve. It is difficult if not impossible to reach a person if we know nothing about them. If we want to connect with people, we must know them for who they truly are.

This is done, he said, by asking questions, lots of them. As you can see in this book, much of our work is framed by good-faith questions that strive to help us better understand our mission field. While reading this book and engaging with American Christian nationalists, I invite you to consider the following:

- ► What do they believe? Value? Hate?
- ► What motivates them?
- ► What gives them honor? Shame?
- ► Who do they see as heroes? As enemies?
- ► What are their rituals? Taboos? Customs?
- ► What are their moral standards? Concerns they elevate above others?
- ► What future do they want for their children?
- ► What deep stories do they tell each other?
- ► What are their hopes? Their ideal future?

Deciphering the answers to these will take some practice. Following this paragraph is a sampling of bumper stickers, posters, and slogans I've collected over the last few years. You have likely seen similar messages in your community. I invite you to study them as if you were a missionary from a different culture seeking to discover answers to the questions above.

- ► "My family and I are protected by the Dear Lord and a Gun. If you intend any harm, you might meet both!" (positioned above a "Jesus is Lord" sticker)

- ► "Jesus is my Savior. Trump is my President." (accompanied by a distressed American flag)

- ► A vintage painting of a European-looking Jesus figure adorned with a red "Make America Great Again" hat.

- ► An image of two AR-15 rifles in the figure of a cross.

- ► "God, Guns, Cops & Trump = America" (next to multiple "F--- Biden" stickers).

- ► "Stand for the flag, kneel at the cross."

- ► "Jesus. Guns. Babies."

Okay, listen, I know that some of these may cause your eyes to roll into the back of your head, but underneath them are values, fears, longings, and hopes. It is easy and unloving to ridicule and mock the image bearers of God who might advocate for these statements. Instead of dismissing them, we can engage them like students of culture, seeking to discern *why* the person believes these messages are valuable. As you read social media posts, engage in conversations, and observe behaviors, prayerfully consider how these messages can help you learn more about the culture you are working to reach as a missionary. As you research your mission field, I pray that you will grow in understanding and compassion.

ARE THEY SAVED?

By framing American Christian nationalists as a mission field I am not arguing that everyone who identifies as such is not saved. People can receive the free gift of salvation through Jesus and still be caught up in convictions that are contrary to the teachings of Scripture. Thanks be to God!

I am, however, arguing that American Christian nationalist leaders are discipling people to adopt theological, cultural, and political commitments that are contrary to the teaching of Scripture. Out of love we can compassionately call them back to the path of truth, the way of Jesus, by using the tools good missionaries use when approaching their mission field. By taking this approach we can wisely and lovingly understand and engage Christian nationalist communities in America.

I also know that *Christian nationalist* can be a type of tribal identity. I have encountered many people who claim to be Christian simply because it is "the American thing to do" but who lack any real relationship with Jesus.

I remember one man I met who bragged about shady business dealings and openly spoke about cutthroat tactics that made him a ton of money while hurting a lot of people. While speaking with this man one day I was shocked to hear him say, "You know preacher, you never know when you are going to die—I'm just glad I'm a Christian."

A Christian! This guy? No way.

He proceeded to tell me about how he heard the gospel years ago; what he took away from the message was that if he said a prayer, he'd go to heaven when he died. He spoke nothing of Jesus or living as his disciple, nor did he exhibit the fruit of the Spirit.

The "gospel" he believes is common in American Christian nationalist circles. It is what some have called "easy believism" or what German theologian Dietrich Bonhoeffer refers to as "cheap grace."[a] This cheap gospel message goes something like this: "God loves you. You sinned. Jesus died in your place. Say a prayer so you can go to heaven when you die."

While elements of this message are found in Scripture, this is not the full message of the good news Jesus proclaimed. It also leads to a type of thinking that understands faith in Jesus as primarily dealing with what happens after I die, not how I live today. It fails to capture the heart of discipleship—following the radical way of Jesus in our daily lives.

The Scriptures call us to make disciples and teach people to follow Jesus' way (see Matthew 28:19). This call to repentance and Christ-centered discipleship is a message for believers and nonbelievers alike.

---

[a]Bonhoeffer writes, "Cheap grace is grace without discipleship, grace without the cross, grace without Jesus Christ, living and incarnate." Dietrich Bonhoeffer, *The Cost of Discipleship* (New York: Touchstone, 1995), 37.

THE RISE OF MODERN AMERICAN CHRISTIAN NATIONALISM

I remember watching the events of January 6, 2021, unfold.[1] Like many, I was overwhelmed by the sheer amount of Christian imagery among the crowd. It horrified me to watch people who had stormed the capital praying to Jesus on the floor of the Senate. What shocked me most was the number of people I knew who were *not* gutted by the day's events.

At some point I denounced these acts of violence and quoted some of Jesus' teachings. The amount of pushback I received from people who said those who attacked the Capitol followed the Lord was discouraging. They were convinced that the day's violence was not only justified but also an act of godly patriotism.

In the days that followed I heard friends, media outlets, scholars, and podcast hosts refer to something called *Christian nationalism*. I don't remember hearing the term before that day, but it seemed bad. As a pastor in a mostly politically conservative community, I had been concerned with the conflation of Jesus with right-wing politics for years. I had followed far-right evangelical politics from the Tea Party movement that arose during the Obama administration on through to the MAGA movement that was now running full-steam ahead. In that decade I do not recall ever hearing a political leader self-identify as a Christian nationalist. Now, it was all over the news.

Turns out, *Christian nationalism* is a term that has been used by scholars since the mid-1900s to describe the synthesis of Christianity with modern politics. In recent years, the term *Christian nationalism* has been appropriated by multiple elected officials, social media personalities, musicians, pastors, and theologians to describe themselves or their views on government and the church.

▶ American Christian nationalism has become a mainstream issue in the political arena. US Representative Marjorie Taylor Greene (R-GA) began selling shirts with the words "Proud Christian nationalist" and encouraging her constituents to purchase them so they can stand against the "Godless left."[2]

▶ The integration and prevalence of American Christian nationalism within our culture at large has increased dramatically in recent years. In 2023 a survey by the Public Religion Research Institute reported that many evangelical Americans hold to Christian nationalist ideas.[3] Additionally, the Google Ngram Viewer (an online tool that displays the frequency of words or phrases over time using digitized book data) shows a substantial rise in the presence of the term *Christian nationalism*.[4]

▶ Prominent figures within the church have become comfortable associating with American Christian nationalism, even helping to advance its cause. Musician and former Bethel Worship leader Sean Feucht said that he is a Christian nationalist.[5] Further, a group known as the Council on Christian Nationalism authored "The Statement on Christian Nationalism and the Gospel," which promotes a form of American Christian nationalism.[6]

▶ Pastors and other notable figures have used their credentials to write books attempting to synthesize the tenets of American Christian nationalism with those of our democracy. Founder and CEO of social media platform Gab.com, Andrew Torba, and Pastor Andrew Isker, who pastors Fourth Street Evangelical Church in Waseca, Minnesota, published a book called *Christian Nationalism: A Biblical Guide for Taking Dominion and Discipling Nations*. Another example is Stephen Wolfe's book, *The Case for Christian Nationalism*, which uses Scripture to build a theological argument for Christian nationalism in America.

Christian nationalism has been gaining popularity in public discourse in recent years, exploding into view with the events of January 6. The events of that day were their own apocalypse, with the cover being pulled back on America to expose the pervasiveness of Christian nationalism—in our government, our churches, our workplaces, and even among our friends and families. While the term is notoriously fluid in its use today, we will now explore its core meaning.

DEFINING OUR TERMS

As students of culture we need to define a few terms that will be crucial for our understanding. These are terms commonly used, misused, or misunderstood when speaking about American Christian nationalism. By clearly defining our terms we can better comprehend the dynamics at work in our mission field.

What is a Christian? Consider the word *Christian*.[7] It is an English translation of the Greek word *Christianos*, which at its core means "belonging to" or "giving allegiance" to Christ.[8]

In *Studies in Jewish and Christian History: Part Three*, Elias Joseph Bickerman writes, "Greek terms, formed with the Latin suffix -*ianus* . . . express the idea that the men or things referred to, belong to the person to whose name the suffix is added."[9] You may have heard of a political group mentioned in the Bible called the "Herod*ians*." These were people who gave allegiance to Herod. They identified themselves with him and followed his lead. A Christian therefore is one who belongs to Jesus; their ultimate allegiance is given to Christ, they submit to his authority and follow his lead.

What is nationalism? To understand nationalism we first need to understand what a *nation* is. A *nation* is a group of people who identify themselves as a nation.

What makes them a nation? Whatever they say it is.

When considering what exactly makes a people into a nation, international political scientist David Koyzis observes, "An answer to this question is not so easily forthcoming, and we are likely to be impressed by the sheer diversity of definitions for *nation*."[10] Throughout history people have chosen to group themselves by things they feel they have in common. Koyzis says this could include things like a "shared language, ethnicity, religion, culture, customs, ancestry, race, homeland, history and constitutional order."[11] There are many things that people choose to identify as the thing that binds them together, but so far no scholar has discovered one single way to determine what makes a people group a *nation*.[12]

In America we have identifiable people groups (nations) that exist as part of our country, such as Cajuns, Cherokee, Pennsylvania Dutch, Southerners, and Yankees. We sometimes even use the term when referring to a collective group of people who all support the same school or athletic team, such as "Buckeye Nation" or "Raider Nation."

Simply put, a *nation* is a group of people who share a common identity. The thing that binds them together could be a language, religion, heritage, or any number of things.

What is the difference between a nation and a state? To better understand the difference between a *nation* and a *state*, let's do a quick recap of your high school civics class.

The world today is divided into *states* (often referred to as countries), which are bordered entities that govern a collection of people. States have laws, courts, militaries, and so on.

However, we Americans are weird. We refer to our country as both a *state* (the United States of America) and a *nation* (one nation, under God).[13]

These views are common, but they don't capture the pluralistic reality of America. In a sense, the United States is not "one nation," but rather a *state* comprising a variety of *nations*—people groups that feature observable customs like dance (Maori haka), culinary traditions (Midwestern tater tot casserole), dialect (Bostonian), music (African American spirituals), and other similar practices.[14]

In his book *American Nations* historian Colin Woodard argues this point and highlights our confusion over these terms:

> Americans . . . often confuse the *state* and *nation* and are among
> the only people in the world who use *statehood* and *nationhood*
> interchangeably. A *state* is a sovereign political entity like the

United Kingdom, Kenya, Panama, or New Zealand, eligible for membership in the United Nations and inclusion on the maps produced by Rand McNally or the National Geographic Society. A *nation* is a group of people who share—or believe they share—a common culture, ethnic origin, language, historical experience, artifacts, and symbols.[15]

The United States of America includes a beautifully diverse multitude of cultures and ethnicities. We have very few consistent, uniform customs and traditions. We are a state made up of many different nations.

So, to review (trust me, this matters!):

▶ A nation is a group of people bound together by something they share in common. Nations often have shared culture, music, food, language, practices, taboos, and so on.

▶ A state is a governed entity with borders, government, laws, military, and the like.

▶ Many states around the world are composed of multiple nations (for example, the United Kingdom includes Scots, English, Irish, and Welsh people).

▶ The United States of America is a state composed of a multitude of nations.

Now that we have a better understanding of these terms, we should put them into a historical context—these are not the only ways the world has been divided over time. Throughout history, people have been divided into empires, kingdoms, and city-states, to name just a few.

When Jesus told his followers to make disciples of all nations (Matthew 28:16-20), he did not have in mind *states* but rather identifiable people groups.

NATIONS IN THE BIBLE

In the New Testament the Greek word that is usually translated as "nation" is *ethnos* and is most often used to refer to a group of people that share cultural, physical, or geographic ties.[a]

The book of Revelation paints a scene of the eternal state (heaven) when the city of God descends and reunites with earth, and God and people dwell together in harmony and love (like Eden). One of the differences between the new Jerusalem and Eden is that in the new Jerusalem all the nations (*ethnos*) of the earth will parade their glory before the throne of God (Revelation 21). Jesus does not erase our ethnicity, our tribe, or our family identity on earth or in heaven. He redeems it, elevating the good while reforming the bad. The Bible concludes with a beautiful vision of all the peoples of the earth living in harmony under the rule of King Jesus.

In the early days of the church Christians sought to live in light of this truth in their day-to-day lives. They were often persecuted by the Roman Empire because they gave ultimate allegiance to Jesus instead of Rome. However, the early Christians did not strive to be enemies of the state. Because they gave their ultimate allegiance to Jesus, they were some of the best citizens, seeking to love and serve their neighbors, like Jesus said to do.[b]

About one hundred years after Jesus' resurrection, a letter was written to the Roman leader Diognetus. The letter describes the cultures and customs of the early Christians living in the Roman Empire. In one section the letter shows that Jesus' followers "dwell in their own countries, but simply as sojourners. As citizens, they share in all things with others, and yet endure all things as if foreigners. Every foreign land is to them as their native country, and every land of their birth as a land of strangers."[c]

The early church was composed of a multitude of nations (Jews, Greeks, Scythians, etc.) and lovingly participated in the life of their communities while being totally devoted to Jesus. In doing so, they were a blessing to their neighbors.

[a] James Swanson, *Dictionary of Biblical Languages with Semantic Domains: Greek (New Testament)* (Oak Harbor, WA: Logos Research Systems, 1997).

[b] Rodney Stark, *The Triumph of Christianity: How the Jesus Movement Became the World's Largest Religion* (New York: HarperCollins, 2011), 114-18.

[c] "Epistle of Mathetes to Diognetus," Alexander Roberts and James Donaldson, translators, Early Christian Writings, accessed April 10, 2023, www.earlychristianwritings.com /diognetus.html.

By the eighteenth century some countries, like the United States and France, had democratized, while many others in Europe and Asia organized into empires by the twentieth century. During the Second World War, we saw the rise of the Empire of the Sun (Japan) and the Nazi regime (which sought to reestablish the German Empire or Third Reich), as well as a radicalized Italy (which sought to renew the Roman Empire). It was during this chaotic period, as fascist regimes rose in Europe, that the term *nationalism* took on a new meaning. Leaders like Mussolini and Hitler leveraged patriotism (love for one's country) and twisted it to mean absolute allegiance to the government of Italy and Germany, respectively. This distorted love for one's people morphed into a form of supremacy, which ultimately led to violence against those designated as outsiders, often resulting in government sanctioned attempts at systematic extermination.

If a *nation* is an identifiable people group, what then is *nationalism*? Nationalism elevates *my* people's concerns over the concerns of others, often at the expense of those who are not "my people." In today's world it often includes a belief that the state (government) should work to protect and promote *my people*'s interests. In the modern era nationalism has frequently been posited as an alternative to *globalism*, an ideology that promotes cooperation of countries around the world and focuses on the concerns of the inter*national* community.

What is American Christian nationalism? American Christian nationalism argues that the American state should be run by Christians and should protect and promote the concerns of Christians over others. How this plays out varies among American Christian nationalist groups and organizations that often emphasize differing beliefs and attitudes toward government, history, and culture. If we are to be good students of culture, we need to ask those in our mission field to define what they mean by the term and to, as Stephen Covey says, "Seek first to understand, then to be understood."[16]

What do American Christian nationalists say they believe? In my conversations with members of groups like Turning Point USA and FlashPoint, I have asked what they mean when they use the term *Christian nationalism* and have encountered nine common sentiments.

While every person is unique and likely would add different nuances, these statements capture the majority of the stated beliefs I've encountered and help us understand our mission field.

1. *I want all Americans to follow Jesus.* If by Christian nationalism people mean they want all Americans to become Christian, I'm all in! I think it'd be really good for everyone to follow Jesus. The way of Christ leads to life abundant and everlasting! While some Christians believe this sentiment with the purest of intentions, there are others, though, who want to accomplish this objective by expelling those they believe to be enemies by denying First Amendment rights to those who adhere to other religious traditions. This statement is also often coupled with some of the following tenets, some of which are more harmful than others.

2. *Historically, most Americans have identified as Christian.* While I am not a historian or sociologist, a lot of smart people who write about American history seem to agree that many people living in America since its founding would identify, in some way, as a Christian.[17] The same could be true for many other countries around the world. This does not, however, mean that everyone claiming to be a Christian has lived according to the teaching of Scripture.[18]

3. *America was founded on Christian values.* There are certainly some biblical values that the founders instilled within our founding documents like "All men are created equal." However, these documents are noticeably human-centered. Take a look at the Declaration of Independence. If you have not read it lately, set this book down and read a copy. Notice how infrequently *God, creator,* and *providence* are mentioned. Now notice how many times humans and human action are mentioned.[19] Also note how many times Jesus is mentioned. Zero.

Additionally, the founders emphasized the pursuit of happiness instead of holiness (which Scripture exalts over other pursuits). While some of the Declaration's ideas square with the teachings of Scripture, many of the ideas come from Enlightenment philosophers.[20]

Further, notice that the founders were careful *not* to promote a state-sponsored religion or any form of Christian nationalism, which many of their forebears suffered in Europe.

4. *The government should recognize Christianity as the official religion of America.* The founders were careful to work against this idea of an official American religion and refused to recognize an official religion for the United States. The idea doesn't line up with their original design for our country.[21]

Some think that was a mistake and believe that the church would benefit from official state sanction. While this may be a noble desire, in my reading of Scripture the church does not need government sponsorship for strength. In fact, throughout history, when the institutional church does enjoy government sanction, it often grows spiritually unhealthy, obtaining a large budget and gaining political influence while experiencing little transformative power within the community. In some cases the state church simply becomes a cheerleader of the state.[22] (As I write this, leaders in the Russian Orthodox Church are making public declarations promoting Russia's invasion of Ukraine.)[23]

5. *The American government should oversee and fund the Christian church.* Perhaps the desire to have the government control and fund the church stems from the frequent misunderstanding that the United States was created to be a Christian nation. If Christianity is written into the DNA of our country, so the logic goes, the church should be integrated with the government and receive government funding. While they believe this will strengthen the church, I believe it would weaken it. I can find no instance of state-governed churches thriving long-term. In most cases, partnership with the state ruined the vitality of the church. Historically, many have argued that one of the key ingredients to the relative vitality of the American church has been its separation from the state.[24]

6. *The American government should promote Christian values.* Frankly, I resonate with the desire to have the government promote Christian values. I would love for our leaders to promote repentance, compassion, social justice, self-sacrificing love, care for the disadvantaged, sanctity of life, turning the other cheek, modesty, contentment (antigreed), chastity, faithfulness in relationships, sacrificing our possessions for the needs of others, and the other teachings of Jesus.

However, when American Christian nationalist leaders use the phrase *Christian values*, they most often mean conservative views on gun rights, school choice, reproductive rights, marriage, sexuality, and gender roles. These issues, while important, do not encaspulate the totality of Christian virtue and ethics.

7. *The American government should enforce Christian values.* I believe the intended sentiment here is that America would benefit if our laws were centered on the teaching of Scripture. However, in practice, much of what Jesus teaches cannot be enforced by government agents.

While I appreciate that murder, theft, and dishonesty in legal dealings are legislated against and often punishable by law, I have serious concerns about how our government might enforce confession and repentance, punish idolatry, or legislate the fruit of the Spirit. It is good when governments legislate according to universal principles that apply to all people. When governments attempt to legislate specific religious ethics and practices, it easily gives way to extreme abuses of power in the name of God.

8. *The American government should be ruled only by Christians.* I do believe that many of the self-sacrificing, loving, gracious people who follow the way of Jesus would make excellent public servants. However, I wonder how the state would go about ensuring that those in office are authentically Christian. What kind of test would they need to pass? Do we just take their word for it, or would we need to see the fruit of repentance and piety before they take the oath of office? What if they fail to exhibit Christlike character while in office? Is that grounds for immediate disqualification?

And which version of Christianity would be allowed to serve? Would Mennonites or Armenian Orthodox be invited to hold public office? Given the vast diversity of political convictions within various traditions and local churches, it is difficult to see how this would be practiced without favoring some Christian denominations over others.

9. *God has a unique relationship with America, like his relationship with Israel in the Bible.* While I believe that God has blessed America in many ways, there is nothing in Scripture that suggests it shares anything like the special relationship God shared with ancient Israel. Though it

may sound positive, this sentiment is extremely dangerous. Many governments in human history claimed to have a special relationship with the divine and used that claim to justify great acts of evil. For instance, when states claim special affiliation with God, they frequently view themselves as God's agents and those that work against them as agents of evil, not only opposing their state but opposing God. And evil people, as the thinking goes, need to be destroyed. In my favorite book, *The Four Loves*, C. S. Lewis argues, "If our country's cause is the cause of God, wars must be wars of annihilation. A false transcendence is given to things which are very much of this world."[25]

States claiming to have a special relationship with God are unbiblical, unsafe, and frequently introduce more evil into our world.

We have just explored the self-professed spectrum of beliefs held by our mission field (much of which has also been recognized in national surveys, journalism, and sociological research).[26] While it's helpful to know what followers say their movement is about, it is only one small way of comprehending something as complicated and controversial as American Christian nationalism. This movement is about much more than one's political convictions. It is also an expression of one's cultural identity and their ultimate allegiance.

MORE THAN MERE POLITICS (THE THREE I'S OF AMERICAN CHRISTIAN NATIONALISM)

American Christian nationalism is not merely a political movement or historical understanding of God's role in American history. It also involves cultural and spiritual dynamics that bolster corrupt views of power and foster unjust actions toward others. To better understand its perverse, sacrilegious, and manipulative paradigm, let's look at three core elements of American Christian nationalism: *ideology*, *idolatry*, and *identity*.

Ideology. A *political ideology* is a system of values and beliefs that dictate someone's view of how a government should work. They are often used as the basis for forming political structures. For example, take the political ideology called liberalism (not to be confused with "the liberal left" in America). Liberalism values the rights and liberty of individuals, and so they argue for free markets, the rule of law, and representative democracy.

As a political ideology Christian nationalism argues that Christians should bind themselves together as a nation and govern themselves as a religious nation-state. In America those holding to Christian nationalism believe that Christians should be in control of the government and, to varying degrees, promote or even enforce Christian values. Paul D. Miller, a political theorist, military veteran, and former White House staffer, puts it another way: "Christian nationalism is the belief that the American nation is defined by Christianity, and that the government should take active steps to keep it that way."[27]

This philosophy is designed to ensure that American Christian nationalists acquire and maintain government power. As historian Jemar Tisby notes, Christian nationalism is an "ideology that uses Christian symbolism to create a permission structure for the acquisition of political power and social control."[28] Christian nationalist leaders invoke rhetoric (such as "fighting the good fight" and "putting on the armor of God") and iconography common to most evangelical spaces (such as featuring crosses or images of Jesus on their marketing material) to sanctify their attempts at consolidating power. While some American Christian nationalists maintain a moderate level of tolerance for other religions or the nonreligious, all agree that Christians should be in charge.

CHRISTIAN VALUES

When American Christian nationalists say that our government should promote Christian values, it is important to ask which ones.

American Christian nationalist leaders frequently tell their followers to support leaders who will "fight for Christian values." As a follower of Jesus I believe that it would be a blessing if those in power in our country exhibited and promoted the Christian values of the fruit of the Spirit (love, joy, peace, patience, kindness, goodness, faithfulness, gentleness, self-control). I would love to see our public servants practice the Sermon on the Mount, the Golden Rule, and love as outlined in 1 Corinthians 13.

However, when American Christian nationalist leaders use the phrase *Christian values*, they most often mean conservative views on gun rights, free market capitalism, school choice, marriage, sexuality, and gender roles, some of which aren't even generally accepted as Christian views. In addition, this narrow collection ignores a multitude of other values elevated in Scripture, such as care for the poor and immigrants, social justice, racial justice and reconciliation, and stewardship of the planet.[a]

---

[a]See Ronald J. Sider, *Rich Christians in an Age of Hunger: Moving from Affluence to Generosity* (Nashville: Thomas Nelson, 2015); Eric Costanzo, Daniel Yang, and Matthew Soerens, *Inalienable: How Marginalized Kingdom Voices Can Help Save the American Church* (Downers Grove, IL: InterVarsity Press, 2022); Nicholas Wolterstorff, *Justice: Rights and Wrongs* (Princeton, NJ: Princeton University Press, 2010); Willie James Jennings, *The Christian Imagination: Theology and the Origins of Race* (New Haven, CT: Yale University Press, 2010); and Douglas J. Moo and Jonathan A. Moo, *Creation Care: A Biblical Theology of the Natural World* (Grand Rapids, MI: Zondervan Academic, 2018).

Idolatry. Tim Keller has frequently made the point that *idolatry* is making a good thing an ultimate thing.[29] American Christian nationalism takes pride in and love of America and elevates it to a spiritual level. It merges allegiance to Jesus with allegiance to the United States, often giving the impression that America is pretty darn close to the kingdom of God. In his book *Keep Christianity Weird*, Michael Frost rightly points out that

> the Kingdom of God is like salt and light. Like God, it cannot be contained or walled in to a particular zone. It's not like America is Kingdom-of-God territory and Syria isn't. The very character of God's Kingdom is alternate to the character and values of this world. It doesn't create borders and defend them. It doesn't foster parochialism or insist on pledges of allegiances to particular flags.[30]

America, for all its virtues, is still just a *kingdom of this world*, and kingdoms of this world cannot be the kingdom of God. American Christian nationalism envisions a worldly government that embodies the kingdom of God and thus creates an idol out of the *state*. Instead of trusting the Lamb of God to return and reign on his own time and in his own way, they attempt to force the early return of the kingdom of God through human power.

Identity. For many people in our mission field the term *American Christian nationalism* refers to the tribe they belong to. They commonly invoke Scripture, reference Jesus, and speak of America's Christian heritage. Referring to the religious language used at Christian nationalist conferences, rallies, and social media posts, Professor Matthew Boedy notes, "The constant rhetoric at the rallies serve as identity formation."[31] The commonly repeated words and phrases solidify the boundaries of the tribe.

We often hear American Christian nationalists say that they are working to preserve "our way of life." Usually, this phrase signals a desire to keep one's ethnic expression or culture. In this sense American Christian nationalism[32] functions as a surrogate for *ethnicity*, complete with art, rites, rituals, taboos, and a founding myth, or what sociologists Philip Gorski and Samuel Perry call the "deep story":

> Christian nationalism's "deep story" goes something like this: America was founded as a Christian nation by (White) men who were "traditional" Christians, who based the nation's founding documents on "Christian principles." The United States is blessed by God, which is why it has been so successful; and the nation has a special role to play in God's plan for humanity. But these blessings are threatened by cultural degradation from "un-American" influences both inside and outside our borders.[33]

This deep story serves to form an identifiable people group, a nation. In the pages that follow we'll explore ways to better understand the tribal identity elements of American Christian nationalism. For now I simply want to recognize that American Christian nationalism functions as more than just mixing religion and politics. It is often tethered to the very core of one's being.

In the day-to-day lives of our mission field these three elements— ideology, idolatry, and identity—harmoniously weave together in their hearts and minds. American Christian nationalism is not simply something they believe but is an expression of who they are, who they love, and what their soul cherishes. While I refer to this movement as American Christian nationalism, some from within will refer to it as conservative Christian patriotism, which, it most definitely is not.

CHRISTIAN NATIONALISM IS NOT
CHRISTIAN CONSERVATISM

As we explore Christian nationalism, we must be careful not to conflate it with Christian conservativism. While most Christian nationalist movements around the world tend to associate with conservatism, it is not inherently conservative.[34] In America those who promote Christian nationalism generally align with the Republican Party, but recent academic research has shown it is also growing among Democrats.[35]

While many believe the American public can be divided into religious conservatives and secular progressives, this binary does not reflect reality. For instance, most Democrats identify as Christians, as do the majority of Democratic leaders in Congress.[36] Progressives at large are not predominately secular. While a smaller percentage of Democrats identify as Christian than Republicans, both are extremely religious and majority Christian. On the other side of the spectrum, many within conservative circles align with the thinking of atheist thinkers like Ayn Rand, Thomas Sowell, James Lindsey, and others.[37] Conservatives are not always religious; progressives are not always secular.

In addition, many prominent Christian conservatives have publicly denounced Christian nationalism, such as Michael Gerson, Liz Cheney, Russell Moore, Paul D. Miller, Peter Wehner, and David French. While maintaining conservative views on politics, these Christian leaders have, in turn, been condemned by many American Christian nationalists. I know hundreds of conservative Christians who reject Christian nationalism and are actively working to resist it in their communities. As we seek to understand American Christian nationalism, we must be careful to not see it as synonymous with conservatism, Republicanism, or other political or religious movements.

CHRISTIAN NATIONALISM IS NOT PATRIOTISM

Over the last few years I got into exploring my family tree. I've been extremely blessed to trace many of the branches to the seventeenth century and a few rare ones back further than that. Much of my family has been in North America for almost four hundred years, with one or two Cherokee branches that undoubtedly go back much further. Many of my ancestors crossed the Atlantic during the colonial era. Many served in the Revolutionary War and subsequent conflicts. Some served as members of the federal government. One of my ancestors worked with Ben Franklin to broker treaties with tribes in the New England region.

I am proud of my heritage. I love America.

When I say that I love America, I don't mean that I love our tax system, environmental policies, or Department of Defense budget. When I say that I love America, I mean my home, the places I grew up, the hamburgers, ice cream, sparklers on the Fourth of July, rock-and-roll, and the Dallas Cowboys.

This love for my home became very real for me in 2014. Over the summer I spent a few weeks in Uganda. While I very much loved my experience (and continue to visit when I am able), near the end of my stay, I grew homesick. *Very* homesick. I longed to be back in *my land* with *my people*; talking *my talk*; eating *my food*; waking, sleeping, and engaging with friends on *my schedule*; listening to *my music*.

I love my Ugandan brothers and sisters, but their ways are not my ways. Their culture is not my culture. I longed for home. My longing was not for my government (the state). While I appreciate the political philosophy of a democratic republic, that is not what I was missing. I was missing my country, my people, my home.

I love America. Not the *state*, but the people. The cultures. The ways of being in the world. A patriot loves their country; celebrates its virtues, practices its customs; and, out of love, critiques its failures and repents of its sins when called for. Patriotism in America emphasizes bringing together people around common beliefs; nationalism, by contrast, emphasizes excluding those they view as outsiders.[38]

Nationalism emphasizes total allegiance to one's people group. In practice this often involves a hatred or dismissive attitude toward other cultures, which frequently devolves into an attitude of supremacy (our nation is better than all others). Nationalistic environments often fear outsiders and have a low view of other nations and countries.

Patriotism, on the other hand, is centered on love for your country—the people, the land, the culture. In his book *The Four Loves*, C. S. Lewis argues that patriotism is similar to the love one has for one's family extended out to their community. He states,

> First, there is love of home, of the place we grew up in or the places, perhaps many, which have been our homes; and of all places fairly near these and fairly like them; love of old acquaintances, of familiar sights, sounds and smells. Note that at its largest this is, for us, a love of England, Wales, Scotland, or Ulster. . . . With this love for the place there is a love for the way of life; for beer and tea and open fires, trains with compartments in them and an unarmed police force and all the rest of it.[39]

Contrary to most expressions of nationalism, patriotic love does not imply hate for someone else's people. Whereas nationalism can be characterized by emotions of fear and hatred, patriotism lends itself to feelings of admiration and grace. Lewis continues, "Of course patriotism of this kind is not in the least aggressive. It asks only to be let alone. It becomes militant only to protect what it loves. In any mind which has a pennyworth of imagination, it produces a good attitude towards foreigners."[40] True patriotism is not combative toward others.

In his book *How to Be a Patriotic Christian: Love of Country as Love of Neighbor*, theologian and philosopher Richard Mouw notes that patriotism is "not just about our relationship to specific governmental policies and practices. It is about belonging to a community. . . . Patriotism is an important sense more about our participation in a nation than it is about loving a state."[41] Patriotism is love for one's people, not hate for the other.

Both Lewis and Mouw argue that healthy patriotism is the love of one's country, warts and all. It focuses on the community one belongs to and does not require negative attitudes toward others. Christian nationalism, on the other hand, often elevates a single people group's needs and preferences over others and seeks power to maintain their position. This illusion of supremacy often leads to fearmongering, hatred, and violence.

As students of this culture we have explored how American Christian nationalism is more than just a set of political ideas and preferences. It is a tribal movement sustained by a formidable spiritual force. To truly understand the people we are striving to reach, we must study the religious dynamic of their community and discern the spiritual powers that so profoundly influence them.

3

LEVIATHAN EMERGES

The Spiritual Power
Behind American Christian
Nationalism

As a rival religion, nationalism may seek to conquer Christianity,
or it may seek to co-opt Christianity for its own purposes. To borrow
some imagery from the book of Revelation, as a "Beast," nationalism
may seek to destroy Christianity through the power of the sword.

DAVID A. RITCHIE, *WHY DO THE NATIONS RAGE?*

ONE SUNDAY IN EARLY 2021 I was talking with congregation members in our church lobby after a worship service as they made their way to the coffee and donuts on the patio when something strange happened. A congregant approached me with a flier for an event happening at a church down the street.

"It's a revival, pastor—you *have* to come!"

The paper put into my hands was a promotional flier for Freedom Night, a large monthly gathering hosted by Turning Point USA.

In my years serving as a pastor I have been asked many times to attend politically themed events, some of which took place in local church buildings. These events are usually called rallies.

What was strange to me was that they didn't call it a rally but a revival. That piqued my curiosity. What type of gathering was this?

Later that week I received more invitations from over a dozen congregants to this event. I decided to attend with one of our church leaders to see what it was all about.

After finding a spot in the massive parking lot, we walked past a smattering of Turning Point USA banners that stood against the backdrop of an enormous, beautiful church building. An energetic group of hospitable hosts welcomed us, asked if we needed anything, and ushered us into the lobby. From there, we entered the sanctuary, where thousands of people were taking their seats.

So far, everything seemed like a normal political rally.

Then the lighting in the room changed as a worship pastor took the stage. He asked us to stand and join him in worship. The band, composed of half a dozen twenty- and thirty-somethings, started playing the song *Freedom* by Jesus Culture as people all around raised their hands, clapped in unison, and shouted "Amen!" and "Hallelujah!" as the bass and drums echoed through the massive building.

As we sang, I realized that this was no political rally; it was an evangelical worship service.

When the singing concluded, they took an offering for one of the church's ministries. They invited people who wanted to be saved to pray a version of the salvation prayer. They invoked Scripture, prayed for revival, and encouraged those assembled to be people of faith.

Okay, pause for a minute.

I have been to a dozen or so political events hosted by churches. Whether it is someone running for city council, the county board, or mayor, these events usually start with a member of the host church thanking people for attending and saying something like, "On behalf of Main Street Church, I thank all members of our community for joining us tonight as we hear from candidate Jones."

After other housekeeping items, candidate Jones will usually take the stage and say something like, "Thank you, Reverend Smith, for hosting this assembly. I am here to discuss my campaign and the positions I will take as your mayor." The church and political leaders usually go to great lengths to show clear lines between their respective roles. Because of these experiences, I was astonished when the definitely-not-a-pastor Charlie Kirk ascended the stage and started talking like of a run-of-the-mill preacher.

After a few minutes of introductory statements, Kirk began preaching from Zechariah 4, providing an overview of the first and second temple (with many allusions to Trump being a Cyrus-like figure), even throwing in a couple admonitions to buy from MyPillow.com.

He proceeded to "preach," quoting Scripture and directly tying portions of this ancient text to his various political agendas. Here is a section from the opening part of the sermon:

> "Not by might, not by power, but by my spirit says the Lord. Do not despise the day of small things. Do not despise these small beginnings, for the Lord rejoices to see the work begin, to see the plumbline of Zerubbabel's hand."
>
> What's the difference showing up to the school board meeting that's not going to save the Republic? But Zechariah is like, no, actually that small thing actually really does make a difference. That one email, that one brick that you're gonna put on that second temple actually makes a big difference that the Lord commands us to care about the small things and it has this cumulative impact.
>
> Little did Zerubbabel know, and he was building the very temple that our Savior was gonna walk through. Little did he know he was gonna fulfill that covenant perfectly so that the Son of God could come and fulfill the promises. Now, that temple was destroyed in about 70 AD by Titus and that was also prophesied by Jesus himself, and so it really got me thinking that the enemy tries to get in our ears to tell us that the small things don't matter.[1]

Kirk then encouraged the congregation to apply this text by promoting Trump-supporting candidates, advocating for shows of force at school board meetings, and financially backing select campaigns during the next election cycle.

The "amens" and "hallelujahs" continued from the crowd as Kirk called us to take a stand for God by rejecting Covid-19 mandates, pressuring local government officials, and donating to "fellow Christian patriots" all in an effort to take our city, state, and country back for God.

The religious language and the crowd's response confirmed my suspicion that we were not attending a political rally. No, this was a spiritual experience; we were "having church."

The rhetoric of the speeches, videos, and prayers gave the impression that we were not discussing political policies and preferences but Christian devotion.

The leaders of this event were leveraging familiar worship music and sacred language to seduce their audience into believing that what we were hearing was in line with the teaching of Scripture and the historic beliefs and practices of the church.

Many within the crowd willingly accepted this message, believing their leaders to be godly people who were simply trying to help them make sense of the chaos and uncertainty they experience in the world. This gathering was not primarily political. It was, at its root, spiritual. But it was not God's Spirit at work. No, it was something insidious, beastly, and seductive.

INTRODUCING LEVIATHAN

Before we continue, I'd like to mention two things about the name of this book. First, it sounds like a late 1980s heavy-metal album. On that point, I am quite proud.

Second, it is weird. It seems the only people talking about Leviathan are Dungeons and Dragons groups, political theorists, and that Bible study at your church that has been examining Revelation for the last five years.

I hear you. I get it. But there is a significant reason why I chose this title for the book. The biblical concept of the Leviathan best helps us imagine and understand the supernatural power covertly at work in our mission field.

Let me explain.

Much of the recent work criticizing the rise of Christian nationalism within America fails to appreciate the spiritual undercurrents that empower it. While many American Christian nationalist organizations center their messaging on certain conservative and nationalistic political ideologies, their true power comes from cultivating anxiety in their audience to grow their influence. Operating like a cult, they promise to quell the anxiety and rage they produce by offering safety, belonging, and purpose to those inside the community. As long as one stays with the pack, they will be protected from the evil outsiders.

This method of taking power by promising to defend and propagate a certain way of life is not new. It can be found in every civilization throughout history any time a particular group has felt their way of life is in danger. This menace is more than just a political idea; it is something more significant, spiritual, and ancient.

In their wisdom the authors of Scripture were aware that an evil force such as this existed, one that promised peace and prosperity while feeding on chaos, demanding allegiance, and eventually requiring a sacrifice. They talked about this spiritual power in a variety of ways, often envisioning it as a beastly creature (Genesis 4:7), such as the serpent (Genesis 3:1), the dragon (Revelation 20:2), or Leviathan (Isaiah 27:1).

According to the authors of Scripture, humans can access the power of spiritual forces. Pharaoh, Nebuchadnezzar, and Caesar all were earthly rulers who were understood to have a connection to what Paul calls the *cosmic powers* (Ephesians 6:12). In the Bible we find that political leaders could, and often did, leverage the forces of chaos and evil for military and economic gain. In so doing they were choosing to trust in and surrender themselves to the chaotic and wicked spiritual forces that work against God's good and loving plan. The prophet Ezekiel argues that earthly leaders can be so committed to these evil methods that they become synonymous with the beastly powers (Ezekiel 29:3; 32:2).

(Let's pause for a minute. I know that a lot of this might feel strange. For many Americans these themes are unfamiliar and unexplored. If you are feeling a bit lost in all this Bible imagery and want to do some deeper study, I've assembled some helpful resources at https://disarmingleviathan.com. Now let's get back to Leviathan!)

Leviathan, the mythical ancient sea dragon, was conceived by intellectuals of the time to symbolize chaos/evil, an unruly power that fought against the loving, orderly rule of the Creator God. Leviathan's domain was the sea (or abyss), which Michael Heiser notes

> was a place upon which humans couldn't live. Consequently, the sea was often used as a metaphor for chaos, destruction, and death. The power and chaotic unruliness of the sea was symbolized in both the Old Testament and a wide range of ancient Near Eastern literatures with a dragon or sea monster . . . known as Leviathan.[2]

James Wilson notes that this symbolic Leviathan is portrayed in Scripture in a variety of ways but is most often working against Yahweh (the Lord).[3] In Isaiah 27:1 the Leviathan symbolizes moral chaos.[4] In the book of Job it is meant to describe the primordial chaos of the unordered cosmos; in the book of Revelation Leviathan is presented as the dragon and the beast, which serve as symbols of the chaos/evil power of the Roman Empire.[5]

Early Christians understood Leviathan as a metaphor for evil, a spiritual power that worked to lead people away from God. In the late sixth century an influential bishop of Rome we now call Gregory the Great was leading the church in the shadow of the recently fallen Roman Empire in the West. In his commentary on the book of Job he teased out the ways that Leviathan deceives people. He talks about how Leviathan uses certain methods to mislead religiously devout people who want to do good and different methods for those who seek to do bad. He says:

> Leviathan tempts in one way *the minds of people who are religious,* and in another those who are devoted to this world. It presents openly to the wicked the evil things they desire, but *it secretly lays snares for the good and deceives them under a show of sanctity.* . . .
> For if the wicked were openly evil, they would not be received at all by the good. But they assume something of the look of good,

in order that *while good people receive in them the appearance that they love, they may also take the poison blended with it that they avoid . . .*

[Leviathan] promises what is good, but [it] lead[s] to a fatal end.[6]

Ancient Christians like Gregory the Great knew that even the people of God could be seduced by Leviathan's power, especially when it presented itself as something godly, good, and aligned with the teaching of Scripture. Gregory was concerned that Christians would be deceived into following leaders and powers that present themselves as godly but are secretly working in ways contrary to the kingdom of God. God's people have been at risk of being seduced by Leviathan's power for millennia.

Like the biblical authors, these ancient Christians believed that humans could access Leviathan's power for their own gain. The apostle Paul speaks of deceitful religious leaders as agents of evil who disguise themselves as righteous, saying "Such people are false apostles, deceitful workers, masquerading as apostles of Christ. And no wonder, for Satan himself masquerades as an angel of light. It is not surprising, then, if his servants also masquerade as servants of righteousness" (2 Corinthians 11:13-15). Paul argues that the corrupt leaders who were infecting the church in Corinth were, like the agents of chaos mentioned in Scripture (the serpent, Satan, Leviathan, the beast), disguising themselves as righteous.

Leviathan often recruits good people to accomplish its evil mission by presenting itself as a godly ally. In America this can be seen when influential leaders co-opt Christian rhetoric and icons, claiming to advocate for Christian values (e.g., "right to life," religious freedom) to gain money and power.

Our mission field is caught in a deceptive trap laid by an enemy at work since the beginning of time. They have been seduced by a spiritual force currently being leveraged by corrupt leaders. In his letter to the church living under the Roman Empire in Ephesus, the apostle Paul said, "Our struggle is not against flesh and blood, but against the rulers, against the authorities, against the powers of this dark world and against the spiritual forces of evil in the heavenly realms" (Ephesians 6:12). Ultimately, our conflict is not with humans but with these perverse spiritual adversaries that seduce people to partner with them in producing these evil acts.

Like Leviathan, American Christian nationalist leaders seek to manipulate their followers through fear and subterfuge. In the next section we will explore their most commonly used methods.

LEVIATHAN'S METHODS

1. Distorting God's Word. One of my most cherished possessions is a copy of the New Testament given to my grandfather during his time as a Seabee in the US Navy during World War II. I believe this type of Bible was a standard issue when he deployed. The front cover of this pocket-sized Scripture is made of steel and inscribed with the words "May this keep you safe from harm."

The title of this sacred text is found on the first page: Heart Shield Bible. Underneath the title is my grandfather's name. If you do an internet search for Heart Shield Bible, you'll find pictures of various copies that were used during the war, some with bullet damage, fulfilling its destiny as a shield for its owner.

It means a lot to me that he kept this memento. The value for me is not that it is a copy of Scripture but that it belonged to my grandfather and represents his sacrificial service during World War II. It is, for me, a source of familial and patriotic pride.

However, I sometimes wonder why the government provided New Testaments to soldiers. Did they provide different religious texts to soldiers of other faiths, or was the New Testament the only one issued by the American government?

My grandfather's Bible reminds me that the Christian Scripture is, as historian Mark Noll quipped, "America's Book."[7] Americans have a long history with the Bible, and it has been formative for our country since before the time of the colonies.[8] American Christian nationalist leaders know that the Bible carries rhetorical and spiritual weight and will often use words or phrases from Scripture to substantiate their arguments. It is one of their favorite tools to manipulate their followers.

Weaponizing the Bible. Over the years I have encountered thousands of references to Scripture in speeches, emails, posters, social media posts, fundraising mailers, and bumper stickers. These are often used in ways not supported by a careful reading of the biblical text or, at worst, in ways that directly contradict the teaching of Holy Scripture (a common practice in America's history).[9] When leaders misuse Scripture for power, they are like those that the apostle Paul warned his protégé Timothy about:

> There will be terrible times in the last days. People will be lovers of themselves, lovers of money, boastful, proud, abusive, disobedient to their parents, ungrateful, unholy, without love, unforgiving, slanderous, without self-control, brutal, not lovers of the good, treacherous, rash, conceited, lovers of pleasure rather than lovers of God—having a form of godliness but denying its power. Have nothing to do with such people. (2 Timothy 3:1-5)

Paul says that some people might appear to be godly, but their lives don't match what they are saying. He coaches Timothy to beware that just because someone talks like a Christian doesn't mean they are actually following Christ. They may be people who are using Leviathan's methods of deceiving people by giving the appearance of being good while working toward evil ends.

This principle is illustrated by one of my favorite movies, *The Book of Eli.* Set in the wild wasteland of post-nuclear-war America, the protagonist, Eli (played by Denzel Washington), is on a journey west, carrying a package of immense value.

The antagonist, a local warlord named Carnegie (Gary Oldman) seeks a mysterious, unnamed book that he believes has great power. He sends raiding parties to hunt down a copy, hoping to use it to solidify his power and expand his influence.

Carnegie: I need that book. I want that book. I want you to stay, but if you make me have to choose, I'll kill you and take that book.

Eli: Why? Why do you want it?

Carnegie: I grew up with that book. I know its power.

In another section of the movie, Carnegie reveals his motivation for obtaining the book to his second in command, Redridge.

Carnegie: [to his men] Put a crew together, we're going after him.

Redridge: For a . . . book?

Carnegie: *It's not a . . . book! It's a weapon!* A weapon aimed right at the hearts and minds of the weak and the desperate. It will give us control of them. If we want to rule more than one small . . . town, we have to have it. People will come from all over, they'll do exactly what I tell 'em if the words are from the book. It's happened before and it'll happen again. All we need is that book.[10]

As it turns out, the book he seeks is the Bible (gasp!). Oldman's character wants a copy of the Bible to use its words to gain power and influence over his subjects. He does not wish to point people to Jesus. He does not desire to gain godly wisdom for himself. He wants to use the words within to manipulate the people he seeks to rule. Unfortunately, this is not a phenomenon that happens only in the movies; this is a tried-and-true practice used by all sorts of movement leaders who twist and manipulate the Scripture to fit their intended outcome—namely, deceive their audience and bolster their power.

One of Leviathan's earliest tricks is distorting God's words to gain power. In Genesis 3 the serpent (which Revelation 12:9 equates with the great dragon) distorts the words of God to manipulate the humans. The serpent says, "Did God really say, 'You can't eat from any tree in the garden'?" (Genesis 3:1). Biblical scholars have noticed that the serpent intentionally misquotes the words of God. Notice the serpent subtly said, "any tree," whereas God had said not to eat from one specific tree.

The serpent did not come at the humans with a straight-up lie; it came with a slight distortion of God's word. For the serpent this has the value of sounding like something God would say, adding weight to its rhetoric. The humans, now deceived, believe that following the serpent will lead to good things. Sadly, in the end, the way of the serpent leads to disruption, disconnection, and death.

In practice we can often tell when God's words are being twisted by observing whether the hearers are experiencing peace, union with God, and unity with each other, or if they are marked by outrage, anxiety, and divisiveness. Leviathan knows what humans want, and appeals to these desires to deceive them.

In the early days of Jesus' ministry the Spirit of God drove him into the desert, where he faced a test. While the first humans were tempted in the safety of the lush garden, the ultimate human is now being tempted in the wild wasteland.

While in the wasteland, the tempter tries to deceive Jesus. Once again, the evil one uses God's words to deceive. This time, the serpent appeals to Jesus' core desires. Notice the three ways Jesus is being tempted. The Gospel of Matthew states:

Jesus was led by the Spirit into the wilderness to be tempted by the devil. After fasting forty days and forty nights, he was hungry.

The tempter came to him and said, "If you are the Son of God, tell these stones to become bread."

Jesus answered, "It is written: 'Man shall not live on bread alone, but on every word that comes from the mouth of God.'"

Then the devil took him to the holy city and had him stand on the highest point of the temple. "If you are the Son of God," he said, "throw yourself down. For it is written:

'He will command his angels concerning you,
and they will lift you up in their hands,
so that you will not strike your foot against a stone.'"

Jesus answered him, "It is also written: 'Do not put the Lord your God to the test.'"

Again, the devil took him to a very high mountain and showed him all the kingdoms of the world and their splendor. "All this I will give you," he said, "if you will bow down and worship me."

Jesus said to him, "Away from me, Satan! For it is written: 'Worship the Lord your God, and serve him only.'"

Then the devil left him, and angels came and attended him. (Matthew 4:1-11)

All three of these temptations speak to the core human needs of safety, belonging, and purpose. Jesus is promised that he will have enough food, be safe from harm, and gain dominion over the whole world if he embraces Leviathan's power and methods. He is tempted to obtain good ends by evil means. American Christian nationalism uses Scripture to advocate for many great things like safety, belonging, and purpose, but it does so by twisting Scripture and arguing that because the ends are good, any means are acceptable. In this regard they advocate not for the way of Jesus, but for the modern political calculus of "the ends justify the means."[11]

Hermeneutical magic. My friend James Nwobu speaks of "hermeneutical magic" (hermeneutics, as you may know, is the art of interpreting Scripture). He says that magicians rely on distraction and sleight of hand to accomplish their goals. They are skilled at directing your gaze where they want so that they can achieve their deception. In the same way American Christian nationalist leaders use Scripture to misdirect the attention of their audience.

I have seen this happen many times, and it often involves boldly misquoting Scripture by strategically replacing one or two words to change the meaning of a text or ripping a text out of context and applying it in a way that the original authors would never have advocated.

Throughout Scripture we find cautions given to the church to discern and avoid these deceitful teachings. The apostle Paul tells his protégé Timothy that "the Spirit explicitly says that in later times some will abandon the faith and follow deceiving spirits and things taught by demons. Such teachings come through hypocritical liars, whose consciences have been seared" (1 Timothy 4:1-2).

One example of hermeneutical magic is *proof-texting*. Proof-texting is the practice of quoting Scripture with little to no regard for its original context to prove one's argument. Often, the verses are used to give the illusion of divine power to a point, but they rarely withstand the scrutiny of thoughtful biblical study.

Proof-texting is common within the American evangelical church, often found on social media, in rally speeches, and on bumper stickers. One of my favorite examples comes from a political rally I attended in 2022. An advocate for American Christian nationalism cited Exodus 20:15, saying, "The Bible says, 'Thou shalt not steal.'" He then proceeded to say, "Therefore, capitalism, which promotes the protection of personal property, is the godliest form of economics." The original hearers of Exodus 20:15 would have never thought about capitalism since it wasn't yet invented. The speaker didn't seem to care about the original intent of the text; instead, the text was ripped from its context and used to support claims about American fiscal policy.

Consider the following list of voting priorities frequently seen online or in chain emails. Notice how the Scripture citations are next to each statement, giving the impression that each phrase is the legitimate application of the text. Notice too what is absent: any Scriptures relating to care for the poor, immigrant, widow, prisoner or orphan, or texts that speak about the responsibility of leaders to have moral integrity.

HOW I WILL VOTE IN NOVEMBER

- ► I will vote for the most pro-life candidate because God hates the shedding of innocent blood (Proverbs 6:17).

- ► I will vote for the most pro-Israel candidate because God blesses those who bless Israel and curses those who don't (Genesis 12:3).

- ► I will vote for the most pro-debt-reduction candidate because the borrower is a servant to the lender (Proverbs 22:7).

- ► I will vote for the most pro-work candidate because God says if a man won't work let him not eat (2 Thessalonians 3:10).

- ► I will vote for the most pro-marriage candidate because God is for marriage as defined in the Bible (Genesis 2:24).

▶ I will vote for the candidate who most closely believes the government's purpose is to reward good and punish evil (Romans 13).

▶ I will vote based, as close as I can, on God's Word (2 Timothy 3).

Sadly, this practice has been part of America's culture since before the Mayflower dropped anchor in Cape Cod. In the sixteenth and seventeenth centuries, the Spanish, Dutch, French, and English immigrants arrived in what is now called America to lay claim to a land they believed they had a divine right to take (see the Doctrine of Discovery[12]). Anglicans, Calvinists, Congregationalists, and Catholics all invoked Holy Scripture to justify their presence and eventually the forced removal of native inhabitants and chattel slavery.[13] When God's word is distorted for personal gain, people get hurt and evil grows.

2. Anxiety and rage. The cultures of American Christian nationalist organizations are marked by anxiety and outrage. As Dave Verhaagen notes, Christian nationalists are "afraid of terrorists and immigrants and Marxists. They are afraid the country is going to hell. They are afraid their children will be morally ruined. They are afraid they will be persecuted for being a Christian."[14]

Their illustrations, stories, and allusions are designed to provoke these feelings, which are easily turned into rage. These organizations frequently raise the topic of the end of the world, end times, or Armageddon, which were made famous in many American evangelical circles by books like *The Late Great Planet Earth* and the Left Behind series.

In these works of fiction the scary antichrist is a globalist or liberal socialist who wants to take over the world and eradicate America and the church. The enemy is often synonymous with the Soviet Union, communist China, the United Nations, or other global actors.

These movies and books have been instrumental in shaping the imagination of American evangelical Christians. When they hear leaders speak of the antichrist and directly tie it to "demonic Democrats" or "Luciferian liberals" they imagine that they are in the end times, battling for the soul of America. They view themselves as the righteous remnant fighting off the armies of evil who have become manifest in the political left. A typical response to the fear of "evil big government" is to take up arms and fight for "the truth."

I have seen this at work in many ways, including some training calls for coaches of "Biblical Patriotism," hosted by Patriot Academy (www.patriotacademy.com). One of the sessions I joined focused on firearm training and featured an instructor giving an overview of the upcoming "Constitutional Defense" gun-training program.

During the Q and A, one of the participants asked specifically about knowing when to use firearms against the authorities. During this training call (for a "biblical citizenship" class), his question was, "When do I shoot government officials?" He was deeply concerned that the evil big government would raid his home and take his children. He referenced a situation in Oregon that many on the call seemed to know about where he claims this happened.[15]

American Christian nationalist leaders leverage end-times anxiety and call their hearers to arms, claiming that aligning with their movement is synonymous with joining the "righteous army" in this end-of-the-world battle of good over evil. In this way the political left is imagined as minions of the antichrist, not neighbors who vote differently.

Why are American Christian nationalists so anxious? Early in my research of the American Christian nationalist movement, I noticed that the leaders and organizations were leveraging language that stoked feelings of fear and anxiety. Angela Denker sees that many conservative evangelicals believe that "American Christianity [is] under siege, resulting in a defensive pushback. Churches today must defend not just Jesus but also America. The American and Christian flags are posted side by side in sanctuaries across the country, often directly in front of the cross."[16]

But what is the anxiety about? What made everyone so afraid? I came to discover that many people were choosing to align with American Christian nationalist organizations because they were fearful of ethnic erasure.[17]

They are afraid that evil people are working to eradicate their way of being in the world, their culture, and their ethnicity. The enemy ("the woke mob," "the demonic left," "antichrist Democrats," "immigrant invaders," "foreign powers," etc.) wants to erase God-fearing, patriotic, hardworking American families. Scholars often refer to this as the "Great Replacement," a theory that has led to domestic terrorism in the United States.[18]

American Christian nationalist leaders tell them that the people who promote views associated with the opposing political party are "out to get you" and are working tirelessly to eradicate "real Americans." They are afraid not only of losing something they love but also of no longer being able to exist in the world.

Ethnic erasure. Ethnic erasure, sometimes referred to as "ethnic cleansing," is a diabolical phenomenon in which one group of people view an ethnic other as a threat to be eliminated. We have seen this phenomenon throughout human history.

► The Romans attempted to erase the Carthaginians.

► The Turks attempted to erase the Armenians, an act which begat the word *genocide.*

► The Nazis attempted to erase the Jewish people.

In the case of Nazi Germany it is important to note that it was the "true Germans" (or Aryans) who wanted to cleanse the country of the *ethnic other* (Jews and others), even though many of them were fellow Germans!

Ethnic erasure does not always include genocide. It can also involve cultural whitewashing. In America we find ethnic erasure in the Native American assimilation movement of the nineteenth and twentieth centuries, which worked to remove the Native people's identity and make the Native people "real Americans" (i.e., White people) through forced removal from their lands, indoctrination at boarding schools, and extreme pressure to assimilate.

American Christian nationalists are afraid of losing their way of being in the world. The slogan *Make America Great Again* illustrates the point. Those fearing the loss of their ethnicity will follow a leader who promises to lead them back to a position of dominance and safety. Many within the movement will do anything, including violence, to protect themselves.[19]

Angela Denker notices how this fear of ethnic erasure drives people to engage in culture wars, saying,

> Their fear, mixed with the sense that they are losing, results in a toxic, jingoistic stew. They were losing the culture wars, losing the young people at church, losing popular opinion, so things like actual church attendance and Bible knowledge mattered less than a politician's ability to catalog their list of perceived cultural wrongs and manufactured fears, like transgender persons using middle-school bathrooms or caravans of unruly migrants storming the southern border.[20]

American Christian nationalists feel like they are at risk of being erased, and they view the bullying, rage, and even violence that marks the movement as justified in order to protect themselves.

Cultural change. While ethnic erasure is a genuine phenomenon, it appears that American Christian nationalist leaders are stirring up fear and anxiety due to people's exposure to other cultures within the diverse communities of America. In his work studying the German church's response to the rise of the Nazi Party, Ryan Tafilowski, a professor at Denver Seminary, once commented to me that "fascism grows in the seedbed of anxiety about pluralism."[21]

America is a pluralistic society. It includes many different cultures bound together not by a common ethnicity or heritage but by a set of political ideals (democratic republic, by the people for the people, etc.). By design it is multicultural. Over the last century we have seen dramatic growth in the diversity of cultural expressions in America, which can feel threatening to those who imagined that their cultural expression was what it meant to be a "real American." This discomfort is being leveraged by American Christian nationalist leaders who interpret this growing diversity as an imminent threat, often painting those outside of their circles as an enemy to fear.

MOURNING THE LOSS OF A CULTURAL EXPRESSION

The pain of the loss of a cultural expression is real. Many of us lament changes in our community. Our favorite restaurant that closed, a band that no longer tours, a sports team that moved to a new city, a historic building that was torn down to make way for something new. These are real losses, and lamenting them is often healthy and good. As a missionary I encourage you show solidarity with those in your mission field.

There may be occasion where the lament experienced is due to a *perceived* loss, perhaps an idealized memory of the past, something that did not truly exist. Consider this statement: "When I was growing up, you could walk to the ice cream shop and not worry about being abducted." While they may not remember or be aware of the crime in the area, they still *perceive* a loss. The pain is real, even if what was lost is misremembered. Real pain invites us to real solidarity, regardless of how valid we feel the loss is.

Anxiety makes us easy to manipulate. Fear can be a good thing. It is what we feel when we are unsafe. Consider your surroundings as you're reading this. Look around. Do you see any bears? If you did, the emotion you would most likely feel is fear. This feeling of fear is what would motivate you to seek safety.

Anxiety is an unfocused sense of fear about an uncertain or unrealized threat. Anxiety is what we feel when we are constantly imagining that a bear is around every corner. When we get a whiff of a strange smell, we think, *bear*!

"Is that bear fur there?"

"Did you hear that! I'm quite sure that is a bear in the kitchen!"

Whether you use the term *anxiety*, *paranoia*, or simply *fear*, when we are in this type of state, we become easily manipulated. It is in the financial interest of Bear Protection Incorporated to keep us in a constant state of anxiety about the imminent threat of the bear army that an evil billionaire is funding to invade our country so they can sell us more Bear Protection Spray.

Followers of Jesus are not called to live with a "spirit of fear" (2 Timothy 1:7 NKJV) but to place their faith in the power of Jesus. Author

Philip Yancey once said that faith in God is "paranoia in reverse."[22] Leviathan thrives on anxiety and paranoia. Jesus calls us to peace, faith, and trust in him.

3. Us and them. One of my favorite albums is Pink Floyd's *Dark Side of the Moon*. One of their quintessential songs laments the frequent practice of dividing the world into *us* and *them*. Often, the *us* group is safe and the *them* group is unsafe. *They* are to be viewed with suspicion as they are likely our enemies who seek to destroy us.

This us-and-them phenomenon is common to all communities and is acutely leveraged by American Christian nationalist leaders who argue that Americans who are outside of their circles are enemies seeking to destroy true patriots. I have heard it parroted by many in our mission field:

- ▶ The candidate I don't like hates real Americans!

- ▶ Those people want to destroy us!

- ▶ The neighboring governor is making it illegal to vote conservative!

American Christian nationalist leaders embellish stories, fabricate scenarios, and frequently outright lie about the nature of those in the *them* group. Functionally, this creates an imagined enemy, a big, bad, scary, monster who is out to destroy us. This monster also creates a useful scapegoat for all the problems we face.

Scholars have noted that tyrants like Hitler and Mussolini garnered immense popularity because they made complex things simple. They blamed their people's pain, frustration, and failures on *them*. Consider the complexity of American economics. Imagine that last month the local factory shut down and Uncle Frank lost his job. He worked hard, faithfully serving in that factory for twenty years. Now, it is gone. Uncle Frank is now out of work, his home value is dropping, and he has a doctor's appointment next week but no insurance to cover the cost.

Why did the factory close and Uncle Frank lose his job? The answer is complex. It could be supply and demand. A larger company might have bought them out. Whatever the reason, it is likely complicated.

Many of us long for simplicity, and complexity often stirs anxiety. We want someone to blame for our pain. American Christian nationalist leaders leverage this desire by blaming Uncle Frank's job loss on the big, bad, scary monster: "It's the socialists who want to destroy America."

By presenting complex issues as simple, the audience feels empowered. They think they understand and can gain control over the situation and find a solution. In the case of our mission field, all the maladies experienced within American Christianity can simply be traced back to *them*, our enemies who wish to persecute us.

In my decades-long experience with American evangelicalism, I have noticed a frequently repeated trope that Christians are a persecuted minority and that the powers that be (e.g., government, the culture, etc.) are actively seeking to destroy us.[23] Things like coffee empire Starbucks' decision not to use the word *Christmas* on their cups or mass retailer Target's gender-inclusive clothing lines are seen as proof of persecution. Like the biblical characters of Esther and Daniel, many American evangelicals see themselves as the faithful remnant standing firm against the wiles of the evil one.

American Christian nationalists often frame anyone who does not agree with them as evil, demonic, or satanic. Author Alan Noble writes, "Narratives of political, cultural, and theological oppression are popular in evangelical communities, but these are sometimes fiction or deeply exaggerated non-fiction—and only rarely accurate."[24] While it is surely good to oppose evil, this stance is rife with opportunities for abuse, toxic leadership, and deception. American Christian nationalist leaders tell their followers that we should "not believe the lies" of the oppressors (usually "liberal media" or "progressive leaders"). It is difficult to trust such leaders' motives when they are telling people that *only they*, as the leader, hold the keys to the real truth or hidden knowledge (which often brings them a significant amount of money and influence).

Knowing the "real truth" can make a person feel powerful. Fear and anxiety can make me feel powerless. Conspiracies are frequently leveraged to stir up this feeling, giving the impression that we are under imminent threat and exposing the real enemy.

Oppression narratives frame our current moment as if Christian Americans are in a war, constantly under assault by an evil oppressor. If we can defeat our enemies, Christians can live happy, peaceful lives without experiencing resistance. A key problem with this view is that it does not align with the teachings of Jesus, who told us that following him will often involve opposition from the powers of this world (Matthew 5:11).

Conspiracy theories. The Old Testament prophet Isaiah declares,

> Do not call conspiracy
>   everything these people call conspiracy;
> do not fear what they fear,
>   and do not dread it. (Isaiah 8:12)

A pastor-buddy of mine who has served his church faithfully for many years shared a painful story with me about one of his church members. He had pastored this man for over twenty years and knew him to be kind, articulate, educated, and someone who had followed Jesus for much of his life. It was clear that he loved and respected this man.

With heartache on his face, he shared that he recently received a very confusing letter from this man, which started with some very kind words, followed by a long-form rant that included over twenty different conspiracies, including the need for the church to test their water supply because the CIA was poisoning the water to make society more malleable to their influence.

My friend was mystified; how could such an intelligent, kind, righteous man buy into these harmful ideas?

One of the great misunderstandings in our day is that people who believe conspiracy theories are uneducated or intellectually deficient. Conspiratorial thinking does not necessarily stem from an inability to think critically; it comes from a framework of suspicion that seeks to make sense of a complex and often confusing world.[25] In the book *QAnon, Chaos, and the Cross,* Shawn and Marlena Graves note that "conspiracies such as QAnon . . . offer a narrative that helps people understand themselves and their world and yields a strong sense of identity, belonging, and purpose and significance to their adherents in a fractured and fragmented world."[26] When the world as we know it seems to be falling apart, having "secret knowledge" can make us feel powerful and bring comfort to our worried souls, even if the sources are dubious or the ideas contradictory.

Moreover, conspiracy theories can also empower us to dismiss troubling information. Consider the conspiracies surrounding the events of January 6, 2021 (it was Antifa in disguise), the murder of George Floyd, or mass shootings at schools like Sandy Hook (they were not real events but actors playing roles). In each of these events some within American Christian nationalist circles promoted conspiracies that functionally empowered people to ignore the painful problems and instead dismiss them away by exposing the "hidden truth."

4. Demanding allegiance. Christian nationalism demands allegiance. Many Christian nationalists say they love their country. While a healthy love for country (patriotism) is a good thing, it can be twisted into a form of nationalism that leads to blind obedience to certain leaders. Samuel Perry and Cyrus Schleifer notice that "Scholars have long noted the tendency for nationalist sentiment to intensify into a form of blind patriotism, in which citizens exhibit unquestioning support for 'the nation,' either minimizing or outright denying their nation's complicity in injustice."[27]

This blind obedience often takes the form of an unwillingness to critique the failures of one's nation. Perry and Schleifer say, "Such citizens can fail to work for reform within the nation but will instead tend to identify 'outsiders' (either within or outside the nation's borders) as the primary threats."[28] The problem is always *them*!

A regular practice of American Christian nationalism is to demonize people who ask critical questions about America and its history. Anyone who brings up the evil of chattel slavery, Manifest Destiny, or the Chinese Exclusion Act at a Christian nationalist gathering will be viewed with suspicion. Critical statements and questions will be perceived as an act of disloyalty—a lack of true allegiance. This, however, fails to recognize how love works. When I love something or someone but do not give it my ultimate allegiance, I am free to criticize it out of love. Because it is not the ultimate object of my affection, the core of my being is not shaken when I discover its imperfections and impurities.

▶ I love my wife best when she is not the object of my ultimate allegiance.

▶ I love my children best when they are not the object of my ultimate allegiance.

▶ I love my family best when its members are not the object of my ultimate allegiance.

▶ I love my church best when it is not the object of my ultimate allegiance.

▶ I love my country best when it is not the object of my ultimate allegiance.

▶ I am at my best as a husband, father, Campbell, church member, and citizen when my ultimate allegiance is to Jesus.

When I make any of these good things my ultimate thing, it becomes an idol, and we cannot question idols because we may find fault, which would mean that my ultimate allegiance is placed in something imperfect and possibly broken. Thus, I would be on shaky ground. An insecure position.

If my ultimate allegiance is to Jesus, then whenever my marriage, family, church, or nation departs from the way of Jesus, I engage in peaceful, compassionate, yet critical conversation. I do so not because I hate them but out of love and a desire for them to better embody the way of Jesus. In his book *Notes of a Native Son*, James Baldwin says, "I love America more than any other country in the world, and, exactly for this reason, I insist on the right to criticize her perpetually."[29] True love speaks the truth about that which is unhealthy.

Communities committed to American Christian nationalism do not encourage critical questions. In fact, those who ask critical questions or engage in critical conversations about the failures of the group are quickly expelled and labeled as enemies (e.g., Republican in Name Only [RINO], being "woke," or liberal traitor).

WOKE

Since 2020 *woke* has become a term of derision used by many American Christian nationalists to mockingly refer to those advocating for social justice in spaces where they do not believe an injustice exists.

Historically, it was a word predominantly used by African Americans to refer to one who was awake to the injustices of racism. In recent years the term has been invoked in songs, social media, and movies to call for a renewed awareness of racism, as well as sexism and other forms of injustice.[a]

In his 2018 book *Woke Church*, Eric Mason states, "Woke is a word commonly used by those in the Black community as a term for being socially aware of issues that have systemic impact. This social awareness doesn't come from just watching the news or reading history through a traditional lens. Being woke has to do with seeing all of the issues and being able to connect cultural, socio-economic, philosophical, historical, and ethical dots."[b]

Mason goes on to say, "Being woke is to be aware. Being woke is to acknowledge the truth. Being woke is to be accountable. Being woke is to be active. This is the call of God on the church and on every believer."[c] In this sense, being woke is a good thing. It means to be aware of and engaged in correcting the injustice (and subsequent suffering) experienced by communities that the majority culture has silenced and pushed to the margins. When we hear our American Christian nationalists use the term, it is sometimes wise and loving to ask them what they mean by it.

---

[a]See, for example, Erykah Badu, "Master Teacher," *New Amerykah Part One (4th World War)*, Universal Motown, 2008; and *Get Out*, directed by Jordan Peele (Burbank, CA: Universal Pictures, 2017).

[b]Eric Mason, *Woke Church: An Urgent Call for Christians in America to Confront Racism and Injustice* (Chicago: Moody Publishers, 2018), 25.

[c]Mason, *Woke Church*, 32.

The demands for uncritical allegiance by Christian nationalist leaders are not unique. You can find similar behavior in families with addicted parents. The leaders often model the behavior of an addicted parent, and their followers assume the role of their child. When exposed to the dysfunction of their addicted parent, the child, knowing that something is wrong with the behavior, will often ask critical questions of the parent. Abusive addicts frequently respond by punishing the child for speaking up, disincentivizing future questions as they expose insecurity. The child, fearing being expelled from the safety and belonging of the family, learns to cope by fabricating stories that explain away the corrupt behavior.

Those suffering from addiction will often work to ensure that the focus is outside-in rather than inside-out. The addict claims the problem is "out there" while the child knows the problem is in-house. However, for fear of losing belonging in the house, the child begins to agree with the addicted parent, reciting the parent's claims that the problem exists externally, thus creating a space for the toxicity of the addicted parent to grow unchecked.

For instance, imagine that the son of an addicted father invites a friend over to play some video games. The father is stoned, unconscious on the couch, and involuntarily urinates on himself. The neighbor friend asks, "Dude, what's up with your dad?"

The child is faced with a dilemma. Telling the truth will get him in trouble with Dad, who might even kick him out of the family. Staying silent will leave the tension unresolved, both of which cause the child distress, who wants two conflicting things: to make sense of the wrong behavior and to maintain his standing in the family. And so, the child devises a story.

"My dad works a lot so he can provide for us. His boss works him hard. His job is so tough that he is exhausted and falls asleep quickly."

The child's story pins the dad's failure (which is the real problem) on others and makes him into a heroic figure. This fantasy accomplishes the goal of explaining away the bad behavior and helps the child feel more secure in the family.

Communities committed to American Christian nationalism operate in a similarly dysfunctional way. The leadership will often behave in ways that are patently contrary to the teaching of Scripture. When questioned about it, the followers explain away the evil behavior.

Consider the following all-too-common conversation with those in our mission field.

A young woman is talking with her friend about the upcoming election. The friend believes that the American Christian nationalist candidate is the only one who will stand for America and our Christian values. The young woman asks about the candidate's dehumanizing behavior toward women. The friend devises a story (which she likely believes) to make sense of the otherwise bad behavior: "Candidate Jones is someone who speaks his mind. He is defending us. Like a good Marine, he might use some impolite language, but we are in a war against the libs!"

The friend might even use some common catch phrases like, "We are voting for a president, not a pastor." Or, as James Dobson, a famous evangelical leader and founder of Focus on the Family, claimed of Donald Trump in 2016, he is "a *baby* Christian."

Like the child of an addicted parent, the friend knows that if she were to question the leader of the tribe, her belonging to the community (family) would be threatened. So, they externalize the problem, saying things like:

"The liberals are attacking real Americans like you and me."

"The immigrants are threatening our way of life."

"The woke media is corrupting our youth."

The evil they focus on is always being perpetuated by *they* or *them*, an enemy that exists outside of *us*. By shifting the focus from the toxicity within to the perceived enemies outside, American Christian nationalists can prove their allegiance to the cause.

5. False promises. The primary way that Leviathan stirs up anxiety is by claiming that our core needs of safety, belonging, and purpose are under imminent threat. Humans will do almost anything to feel safe, experience belonging, and find a purpose for their existence. Leviathan fabricates or distorts realities to ensure that its hearers feel as if their core needs are at risk and then promises to make the pain disappear by claiming it can provide for these needs.

This is apparent in email newsletters, speeches, video clips, and news-media programs targeting our mission field. If you listen to the rhetoric, you'll hear something like this:

- ► There is a big, scary enemy out there that wants to destroy you, your way of life, and everything you stand for. (Anxiety)

- ► But we [the American Christian nationalist organization] will stand together and watch each other's backs. (Safety)

- ► True patriots like you and me know the truth from the lies. (Belonging)

- ► Now let's get out there and take back our schools so we can protect our kids from the woke demons. (Purpose)

Once a person is convinced that the American Christian nationalist organization or leader is providing them with safety, belonging, and purpose, they will look for ways to confirm the validity of their belonging. They will fall in line to remain in the community. To question the organization or its leadership is to risk their safety, belonging, and purpose. Katherine Hayhoe notes, "For most of us, the value of belonging far outweighs the value of attaining new information, especially if publicly accepting that information and speaking up might lead to a negative outcome—an argument, the cold shoulder, or even ostracism from your social group."[30]

For those within the American Christian nationalist community, repentance (changing their mind and behavior) will often mean that they will have to leave the safety of the community. When we call people to repentance, we must also point them to the ultimate source of actual safety, belonging, and purpose, namely, Jesus. Moreover, we must embody Christ-centered community within our local churches.

More than just a political phenomenon, American Christian nationalism is a toxic tribalist movement seeking to elevate its own using the tools of distorting God's Word, fearmongering, deception, and abusive leadership. As such, they leverage the spiritual power of Leviathan. The

Scriptures show that this form of corrupted power frequently presents itself as good and seduces good people by disguising itself as righteous. While the beastly power promised by American Christian nationalism can be tempting for many, if we take a closer look at its effects throughout history, we can see that Leviathan often offers power to those who are afraid, but in the end its promises are empty.

4

LEVIATHAN EXPOSED

The Emptiness of American Christian Nationalism

WE HAVE EXPLORED THE HISTORY, self-professed beliefs, and core characteristics that define and illustrate our mission field. We then took a deeper look at the powerful spiritual dynamic of this movement. Though American Christian nationalism has been difficult to define, we've learned enough about it to draw some conclusions. In light of many hard truths and evidence that point to a culture that claims to be Christian, we can see with unbiased eyes that, in actuality, it is a group that operates in contradiction to the grace, love, and humility embodied by Christ. The Scriptures call us to a Jesus-centered wisdom that seeks to love God and neighbor. American Christian nationalism instead relies on worldly thinking and self-elevation, often endorsing violence to secure peace and power for their own. We know that neither these ends nor the means are aligned with the way of Jesus. While many in our mission field believe these methods will bring about a God-honoring culture, we can see that Leviathan only produces destruction and cannot deliver on the good that it promises. We will now explore the emptiness of Leviathan's promises.

AMERICAN CHRISTIAN NATIONALISM HURTS PEOPLE

It is a bit of an understatement to say this movement has had a dramatic impact throughout history. The seeds of Christian nationalism in

America have produced the rotten fruit of oppression, segregation, violence, misogyny, bigotry, xenophobia, and murder. Historian Kristin Kobes Du Mez speaks to this:

> The belief that America is God's chosen nation and must be defended as such . . . serves as a powerful predictor of intolerance toward immigrants, racial minorities, and non-Christians. It is linked to opposition to gay rights and gun control, to support for harsher punishments for criminals, to justifications for the use of excessive force against Black Americans in law enforcement situations, and to traditionalist gender ideology. White evangelicals have pieced together this patchwork of issues, and a nostalgic commitment to rugged, aggressive, militant White masculinity serves as the thread binding them together into a coherent whole. A father's rule in the home is inextricably linked to the heroic leadership on the national stage, and the fate of the nation hinges on both.[1]

Groups that imbibe American Christian nationalism often cultivate combative postures toward others, which has resulted in great harm and destruction of communities at large, especially minority and outlier groups that American Christian nationalists feel entitled to exert force over; worse, they feel wholly justified in doing so because they have been fed the lie that their actions are sanctioned as holy and part of God's plan.

In America's history, Christian nationalism has propped up evil cultural beliefs like Manifest Destiny (which led to the slaughter of a multitude of Native Americans, stolen land, and forced displacement) as well as the Mexican-American War.[2] In recent history this movement has been increasingly nurtured by political and religious leaders and continues to be a corrupting influence on the church and the country, hurting countless people worldwide.[3]

AMERICAN CHRISTIAN NATIONALISM RELIES ON THE POWER OF THE SWORD

If Jesus wanted to establish a Christian nation-state, why didn't he kill Pilate? Proponents of American Christian nationalism argue that the church should fight to gain worldly power to promote their way of life and protect themselves from their enemies. Jesus, on the other hand, teaches us that power is to be used to self-sacrificially serve others, even our enemies.

American Christian nationalism calls us to take up the sword. Jesus calls us to take up the cross. The Gospel of Mark records a moment when two of Jesus' closest disciples attempt to grab worldly power:

> James and John, the sons of Zebedee, came to him. "Teacher," they said, "we want you to do for us whatever we ask."
>
> "What do you want me to do for you?" he asked.
>
> They replied, "Let one of us sit at your right and the other at your left in your glory."
>
> "You don't know what you are asking," Jesus said. "Can you drink the cup I drink or be baptized with the baptism I am baptized with?"
>
> "We can," they answered.
>
> Jesus said to them, "You will drink the cup I drink and be baptized with the baptism I am baptized with, but to sit at my right or left is not for me to grant. These places belong to those for whom they have been prepared."
>
> When the ten heard about this, they became indignant with James and John. Jesus called them together and said, "You know that those who are regarded as rulers of the Gentiles lord it over them, and their high officials exercise authority over them. Not so with you. Instead, whoever wants to become great among you must be your servant, and whoever wants to be first must be slave of all. For even the Son of Man did not come to be served, but to serve, and to give his life as a ransom for many." (Mark 10:35-45)

Jesus responds to his disciples' request for worldly power with a call to self-sacrificial love: to take up their cross and follow him. This can be an especially difficult assignment when we are afraid of losing things that we hold dear. In those moments it is tempting to reach for worldly power. Perhaps this is why Peter drew his sword when a mob came to arrest Jesus. John records this scene: "Then Simon Peter, who had a sword, drew it, and struck the high priest's servant, cutting off his right ear. (The servant's name was Malchus.) Jesus commanded Peter, 'Put your sword away! Shall I not drink the cup the Father has given me?'" (John 18:10-11).

Like Simon Peter, American Christian nationalists give in to the temptation to alleviate their fear by reaching for the sword. In his book *The Religion of American Greatness*, Paul Miller notes,

> As conservative White Christians have felt their power ebbing, they have made the preservation of their power itself into their last great moral crusade. America's White Christian ethnoreligious sect has convinced itself that its own power is essential to the nation's future, and, consequently, that preserving its power is a selfless, moral act.[4]

American Christian nationalism calls us to take up the sword, gain more power, and use it to protect and promote our way of life. Jesus calls us to take up our cross and use our power to serve others, especially those who are not like us.

When things seem out of control, when we fear the loss of that which we love, when the pressure is on, will we reach for the power of the cross or the power of the sword?

Throughout Scripture empires like Egypt, Babylon, Rome, and even Israel are called out for succumbing to their lust for worldly influence and might. The kingdoms of *this* world constantly desire sword power. But King David said, "Some trust in chariots and some in horses, but we trust in the name of the LORD our God" (Psalm 20:7).

The people of God are called to put down their swords and trust in the power of Jesus, who establishes his peaceable kingdom by taking the cross on our behalf, rising from the grave, and calling us to live like him.

AMERICAN CHRISTIAN NATIONALISM WOUNDS THE CHURCH

Over the last few decades a multitude of stories have surfaced of clergy engaging in evil practices ranging from deception and embezzlement to sexual assault, pedophilia, and rape. Toxic leadership wounds people, especially in the church. Though often more subtle, the type of *power-over* leadership embodied by many Christian nationalist figures is being mimicked in pulpits across America as many clergy embrace combative, authoritarian, and narcissistic forms of leadership.

Since beginning the Disarming Leviathan project I have heard from over a dozen men and women who served under pastors who were leading their churches into a flagrant pro–Christian nationalist position, often demanding that the staff fall in line or resign. When Christian leaders align with American Christian nationalism and deploy Leviathan's methods to grow their organizations, it wounds the people who are under their care and distorts the witness of the church.

THE STODDARDS' STORY

"In early June 2020, a memo was sent out to the staff of Dream City. It announced that Turning Point Action, the advocacy arm of Turning Point USA, was hosting an event at the church and Trump would be speaking at it. Any questions, the memo said, should be directed to the church employee's supervisor.

"Both Mark Stoddard and his wife, Rachel, who was the church's vocal director, sent emails. They weren't confrontational, Mark Stoddard said. The sentiment was that 'this could jeopardize good work the church has worked years to build.'

"Rachel Stoddard said she ended hers with a request: 'Please reconsider the decision to host this rally.'

"To the public, Dream City Church was saying it was merely hosting the rally, renting it to a tenant that needed a large space. It said the decision to host Trump was not political.

"But, a few days before the rally, Barnett called a meeting of all the staff of Dream City Church over the Zoom video conferencing platform.

"Luke Barnett gave what Mark Stoddard described as an impassioned monologue about the culture wars and how Dream City Church needs to join the fight against an 'existential spiritual threat.' One of those battlegrounds, he said, was politics.

"The pastor then told his staff, according to Stoddard, 'if you are not willing to fight these culture wars with me and you receive a paycheck from this church, I'm asking for your resignation.'

"The Stoddards were astonished at this turn for a pastor who had never asked them about political persuasion before. They resigned.

"So, they said, did a handful of others."

---

[a]Richard Ruelas, "Disarming Leviathan: One Pastor's Fight against the Christian Nationalism," *AZCentral*, November 6, 2022, www.azcentral.com/in-depth /news/local/arizona-investigations/2022/11/04/turning-point-charlie-kirk -distorting-christianity-phoenix-pastor-says/8082545001.

AMERICAN CHRISTIAN NATIONALISM HINDERS EVANGELISM

In 2021 I had lunch with a man who referred to himself as a spiritual tourist and didn't have a faith background. During the conversation, he said something that took me by surprise: "You know, the church has a huge branding problem."

Branding problem? At first I thought he didn't like our church's website or logo or something like that. I asked him to say more. He said that before our meeting, he had watched a sermon from our church that explored the nature of the kingdom of God and how it transcended politics. He was struck by the upside-down nature of Jesus' teaching on power such as "take up your cross" and "the first shall be last."

"My friends and I talk about this kind of stuff all the time," he told me. "Frankly, we have no idea that you guys [the church] are talking about this too." He continued, "My friends and I just think you guys are just in there [the church building] talking about a particular angle of politics and trying to get everybody to fall in line. If we knew *this* [the kingdom of God] is what you were talking about, we'd be there every week. Because this is really attractive." He finished with, "We think that churches are just out there doing political punditry."

Far from seeing the local church as a people committed to following the way of Jesus, he viewed us as conservative political power brokers hell-bent on fighting a culture war. The conversation continued, and he asked a ton of insightful and thoughtful questions about faith, Jesus, and the church.

As we concluded, he said something I'll never forget: "If I come to your church, will I get lynched?"

"What do you mean?" I replied.

"Well, I'm a Democrat. Will I be welcomed in your church?"

Think about that question. This man, a self-identified spiritual tourist who is very interested to learn more about Jesus was concerned that he would be rejected by the church because of his political convictions. The church has a branding problem.

This problem is made worse when local churches align with movements like American Christian nationalism. It's a misstep not reserved for conservatives alone; progressive Christians can also be tempted to conflate their theological beliefs with political allegiance. When religious institutions make such strong political alignments, they bear witness to a false gospel and replace the good news of the kingdom of God with the empty promises of the kingdoms of this world. When churches endorse Christian nationalism, they hinder their ability to reach people from all perspectives with the unconditional love of Jesus.

STATE-SPONSORED TORTURE AND GLOBAL EVANGELISM

How is the witness of the church affected when a country that calls itself Christian goes to war? Consider America's use of waterboarding against people the government identified as enemies. Is this form of torture to be considered a Christian act? And what of the acts of genocide committed by many Western Christians during their wars of expansion and colonialization? Do these acts communicate the love and grace of Jesus to the watching world?

When a state like the United States takes the identity of a *Christian nation* and then proceeds to engage in violence, torture, and assassinations, it distorts the witness of the church, whose head is the Prince of Peace, Jesus, who calls us to lay down our swords and to love our enemies.

C. S. Lewis recognizes the negative impact of states claiming to be Christian on the mission of the church. In critiquing Western governments that leverage Christianity, Lewis states, "Large areas of 'The World' will not hear us [Western Christians] till we have publicly disowned much of our past. Why should they? We have shouted the name of Christ and enacted the service of Moloch."[5]

In the book *A Search for Christian America* Mark Noll and other historians recognize the negative impact of Christian nationalism on the witness of the church, stating, "The idea of a 'Christian nation' is a very ambiguous concept which is harmful to effective Christian action in society."[6]

While states can be composed of many Christians, the state itself is not inherently Christian nor can it act in Christian ways. The state cannot follow Jesus, live out the Sermon on the Mount, or embody the fruit of the Spirit. Moreover, the state is charged with doing things like espionage, warfare, and many other things that are not directly aligned with walking the way of Jesus. When states claim to be Christian, they give the impression that their actions are aligned with the teachings of Jesus and sanctioned by God, thus misrepresenting the witness of the church.

AMERICAN CHRISTIAN NATIONALISM PROMOTES SYNCRETISM

American Christian nationalism is a form of *syncretism*, a term used in seminaries and missionary organizations to describe the practice of syncing or mixing aspects of the Christian faith with local religious traditions, cultural values, or commitments in a way that distorts the gospel.[7]

Examples of syncretism are found in the Bible. For instance, in Judges 17 Israel mixes Yahweh worship with Canaanite religion. Examples today include the Santa Clause figure merged into the Christmas season, the merging of consumerism with Christianity in the prosperity gospel, new-age movements that pick and choose elements of different faiths (sometimes referred to as "cafeteria religion"), or Santeria (a mixture of the Yoruba religion and aspects of Roman Catholicism).[8]

Consider the hymn books you might find at your church building (which, depending on your tradition, may be found in the pews, on a bookshelf in the basement, or on the shelf of your worship pastor's office). In it, you will likely find classic hymns like "Amazing Grace," "Nothing but the Blood of Jesus," and "How Great Thou Art," songs of profound faith, beauty, and theological depth that glorify the triune God and that can be sung by faithful Christians worldwide. But continue to scan the pages and you will also likely find "My Country 'Tis of Thee" and "Battle Hymn of the Republic," songs promoting American values, celebrating nationalistic power, and sung to glorify America. These songs cannot be authentically sung by the global church.

Many of our hymn books syncretize Americana with Christianity by placing songs that elevate the God of Scripture alongside those that praise the power and beauty of America. In the lived experience of the average American Christian nationalist, these are not mutually exclusive but are part of the same religious experience.

Other forms of syncretism can be found in images that merge the American flag with the cross or portions of Scripture etched onto firearms. As pastor and scholar David A. Ritchie argues in his book *Why Do the Nations Rage*, "Nationalism welcomes syncretism, but anathematizes those who would claim absolute allegiance to the one who has been given all authority in heaven and on earth (Matt 28:18)."[9]

POOP IN THE BROWNIE MIX

Some of these expressions of syncretism may feel harmless. What's the big deal if someone has a painting of a Jesus-like figure wrapped in the American flag? What is the danger of hosting a Fourth of July worship service with patriotic songs mixed with worship songs to Jesus? While some of these practices may feel harmless, they run the risk of distorting the gospel by merging authentic expressions of Christianity with the American civil religion.

American civil religion is a term used to describe the religious practices of the American people and includes things like sacred songs like "My Country 'Tis of Thee," decor like flags and Uncle Sam, and liturgical acts like reciting the Pledge of Allegiance or placing one's hand over one's heart during the national anthem.

These can be good things when they are rightly understood as expressions of American patriotism, not expressions of Christian devotion. When American Christian nationalists speak of America as God's country or use imagery of a cross draped in an American flag, they are functionally syncing the two belief systems into one, thus misrepresenting the gospel.

A while back I was talking with a good friend about the corrupting influence of syncretism in the American church. At one point in the conversation, he posed a disgusting but important question: "How much poop in the brownie mix is tolerable before it spoils the whole thing?"

That is gross, but I got his point.

No matter the amount of poop, if any of it is in the brownie mix, the whole batch is ruined. Moreover, if we cook up the batch, the unsuspecting recipients may consume the dessert, unaware of the foreign elements present in the batch. It could make them sick or even worse.

American Christian nationalism attempts to sync two incompatible ideologies, namely, nationalism and the way of Jesus. This often strengthens the position of the nationalist leaders and weakens the witness and fidelity of the church. While some forms of syncretism may seem benign, one must consider how much nationalism can be mixed in with the gospel before it makes people spiritually sick.

AMERICAN CHRISTIAN NATIONALISM CAN LEAD TO EMPIRE WORSHIP

The Scriptures teach that humans are tempted to worship created things instead of their Creator (Romans 1). This includes sex, money, education, family, tribe or ethnicity, military might, and economic security. Elevating these good things above Jesus leads to corruption, fractured relationships, and ultimately death.

One of the ways Leviathan works is by guiding people to worship political power. A common occurrence in Jesus' day was for people to put all their faith in the strength of their empire, or if they were enemies of the empire, a military savior who would overthrow the current regime and establish a new one. In the Gospel of Mark, Jesus told his disciples that "false messiahs and false prophets will arise and will perform signs and wonders to deceive, if possible, even the elect" (Mark 13:22). These false messiahs were often insurrectionists, promising to overthrow the current government and establish a new kingdom through violence.

In those days the Roman Empire was deified, and the leader of Rome (Caesar) was seen as a god. Roman citizens frequently visited temples built to venerate Rome and participated in holy days and feasts designed to worship Caesar as a god. Military power, economic prowess, and artistic expression were all considered proof that Rome was divine. Empire worship was one of the more common forms of idolatry for those living under the Roman Empire. The book of Revelation is a harsh, critical parody of Rome's worldly power and a caution to those who would worship it.[10]

While many Americans don't often think of the United States as an empire, we are easily tempted to glorify our national influence, military might, and economic strength. If you visit Washington, DC, I invite you to do so with the mind of a missionary. As you walk the National Mall, visit the monuments and museums along its path, explore the beautiful architecture, and notice the slogans, icons, and cultural expressions, you may notice many Roman images, Latin phrases, and Greek architecture. If you visit the National History Museum, you will even find a statue of a shirtless George Washington, looking much like Caesar. America has been, in large part, fashioned in the image of Rome. We are not immune from empire worship.

David A. Ritchie notes that empire worship can also be found in our national symbols, stating, "In its doctrine of God, nationalism also tends to personify the nation into a mythical being. As the god Ashur was seen as the spiritual embodiment of the Assyrian empire, so too did modern nations take on the personalities of quasi-deities, such as Uncle Sam of the United States, John Bull of England, or Marianne of France."

While there are a handful of public monuments adorned with Scripture, and the word *God* is referenced on various etchings, the name of Jesus is rarely if ever mentioned in the public spaces of DC.[11] If

American Christian nationalists claim that the United States is a Christian nation, then why does the aesthetic of our nation's capital lean more Greco-Roman than Judeo-Christian?

Symbols of national pride, when used wisely, are means of showing honor and solidarity. They can be a way to celebrate our culture and serve as a reminder of the values of our country. They can also become twisted into a form of idolatry, morphing into venerated symbols and a means of state worship.

AMERICAN CHRISTIAN NATIONALISM PROMOTES TOXIC TRIBALISM

Many prominent advocates for Christian nationalism call on religious leaders to compel their congregations to vote as a bloc, securing government power so that we can protect ourselves from our enemy. The enemy that they are calling us to fight is the progressive left, a group they claim is working to leverage government power to destroy the family, America, and the church. Therefore, they argue, clergy members who do not take a stand are abandoning their post and relinquishing their flocks to the evil one.

Charlie Kirk, the founder of Turning Point USA, often makes this point stating, "Theological disputes are important, but if we don't get liberty, we will be debating about them in prison."[12] If we don't take power, Kirk argues, our enemies will put us in prison, and so taking power by any means necessary is justified. Paul D. Miller notes:

There is a subtle and crucial difference between seeing power as a means to an end, a necessary precondition for pursuing justice, on the one hand, and seeing power as intrinsically good, as if power in the right hands is inherently righteous, on the other. Many White American Christians seem to be gravitating to the latter view of power, the view that the identity of the person who wields power sanctifies its use: Power in the hands of Christians is by definition good and thus the pursuit and preservation of Christian power must be our preeminent goal.[13]

American Christian nationalist leaders like Kirk focus much of their energy on forming their audience into a unified tribe that gives them allegiance, empowers them with funding and manpower, and obeys their commands. These leaders argue that because they are Christian, their cause is just, and you can trust that the ends justify the means. Toxic tribalism elevates loyalty to the tribe above all other values. To question the leader is to betray the tribe.

Many people who study mission work have recognized three primary cultural frameworks that shape people's thinking about themselves and their interaction with others. They are (1) guilt-innocence, (2) shame-honor, and (3) fear-power. In the book *3D Gospel*, Jayson Georges defines them as follows:

- ▶ *Guilt-innocence* cultures are individualistic societies (mostly Western), where people who break the laws are guilty and seek justice or forgiveness to rectify a wrong.

- ▶ *Shame-honor* cultures describe collectivistic cultures (common in the East), where people shamed for not fulfilling group expectations seek to restore their honor before the community.

- ▶ *Fear-power* cultures refer to animistic contexts (typically tribal or African), where people afraid of evil and harm pursue power over the spirit world through magical rituals.[14]

While multiple frameworks can be found in all societies, most favor one over the other two. American Christian nationalist organizations tend to prioritize the *fear-power* dynamic, which is common to tribal cultures. Miller sees this at work as well, noticing that "Christian nationalism is, in effect, identity politics for tribal evangelicals." He goes on to argue that modern evangelicals act "like a cultural tribe . . . advocating for its own power and protection, rather than a people from every tribe and nation advocating for universal principles of justice, flourishing, and the common good."[15] American Christian nationalism functions as a tribal community committed to its own advancement over others and is led by leaders who stir up fear of *the enemy* and promise safety if we give allegiance to the leader of the tribe.

Our mission field is inundated with messages that leverage the *fear-power* framework, such as "we are losing our country," "we are under attack," or even "there is a secret cabal pulling the levers of power." To be accepted by the tribe, a person must agree with and repeat these talking points.

Another common element of tribalism is the worship of ancestors. In American Christian nationalist circles, America's founders are often treated as semi-divine figures who wrote holy texts and were uniquely empowered by God to shape the foundation of the United States. To question the founders is to question God's anointed ones.

For our mission field, venerating ancestors, proclaiming the right politics, and avoiding taboos are more about belonging to the tribe than about fidelity to the teachings of Jesus. Angela Denker recognizes this in her work *Red State Christians*:

> Most of all, they were desperate to reclaim the idea that America was a uniquely and especially Christian nation, where your culture—your positions on social issues, your views on gun control and abortion—were much more important than your grasp of theology or your understanding of grace, death, and resurrection.[16]

Our mission field operates like a tribe fearing the enemy and trusting in their leaders for safety. The tribe only works if everyone supports the leader. Dissent could mean destruction. And so they work to protect the tribe by bolstering the tribal leaders.

AMERICAN CHRISTIAN NATIONALISM THRIVES ON BORROWED CONVICTIONS

As a pastor I frequently hear about the decline of biblical literacy and engagement.[17] While many in our mission field have a high view of the Bible, most rarely study it. Instead of wrestling with Scripture in a local church community, many choose to borrow the biblical convictions of their favorite authors, celebrity pastors, or political leaders without deep meditation, personal experience, or thoughtful engagement.

Learning from others is often a good practice. Throughout the history of the church Christians have developed their convictions assisted by the teachers who have come before them. In some traditions this takes the form of catechesis or a series of classes required before someone is baptized. In Scripture we see the apostle Paul encourage his protégé, Timothy, reminding him that he has become convinced of the faith he learned from older saints, including his mother and grandmother (2 Timothy 1:5). These are *learned* convictions. *Borrowed* convictions, on the other hand, are adopted by someone simply because they favor the person presenting them. American Christian nationalist leaders have capitalized on this trend by presenting their arguments as being "Bible-based," and then demanding their followers to uncritically adhere to and repeat them, which many of them obediently do.[18]

Over the last decade I have been in the process of disentangling my actual convictions from those I have borrowed from my favorite leaders, scholars, and mentors. I have found that many of my perspectives on theology were acquired secondhand. I accepted many of them uncritically, without engaging the Scriptures myself. It reminds me of when I was with my then-boss Pastor Rick. One day we were driving to the Black River in northeastern Arizona to do some trout fishing. During the car ride, I asked Pastor Rick, "Are *we* Reformed?" He responded graciously, asking me what I meant by *Reformed*.

Being Reformed means something significant. It is a term used to describe a specific theological tradition that dates back to the sixteenth century. Many leaders, scholars, and authors from the Reformed movement have provided profound spiritual guidance, theologically rich commentaries, and powerful Jesus-centered sermons.

The problem is, at the time, I had no idea what it meant.

I was not asking Rick if *we* were Reformed because I was wrestling with my convictions. I was asking because I wanted to ensure that our church was not in the wrong tribe. I didn't know what being Reformed meant; I just knew I wanted to *be* Reformed because all the cool leaders I looked up to said *they* were Reformed. And I wanted to be like them. I had not thought deeply about Reformed theology; I just loved the feel of the movement, which had been referred to as "young, restless, and Reformed."[19] I was both young and restless, and it felt good to belong to a movement like that. It also gave me a community to belong to. And I wanted to belong. Frankly, I was still pretty new to conversations about doctrine and theological systems. I could not have articulated what it meant to be Reformed, but I knew I wanted it.

I would argue with my peers, mimicking the talking points I picked up from the movement's leading pastors, authors, and scholars. With vigor and confidence I would quote from books that I never read. I would criticize "heretics" on the opposing teams I'd never engaged with. If the leadership said they were the enemy, well, then they were *my* enemy! Adopting these attitudes made me feel like I belonged.

As the years went by, my circle of friends expanded, and with that, the pastors, theologians, and leaders they introduced me to. I discovered different ways of approaching the Scriptures and other methods for putting them into practice. In the process I found that some of what I believed would not fit in with the Reformed movement that I identified with. This was scary.

If my convictions were not aligned with being Reformed, would I be kicked out of the tribe? Would it hurt my career? I feared I would no longer be welcomed into certain spaces or groups. I wouldn't be invited to the cool pastor club. (No, this does not exist—at least, I don't think it does—or maybe it does exist, and I've never been invited. I'll ask around and let you know.)

Moreover, I did not want to be the "enemy" of the people I looked up to. I heard how some of them talked about those outside the tribe. They were people who didn't stand for truth, didn't take the Bible seriously, or were given over to the godless culture. I didn't want them to think of me that way.

This is the perilous road of discovering one's own convictions. Changing our minds might cost us job offers, accolades, and even community. While they might make us feel safe, borrowed convictions do not satisfy. When the reality of life hits, when we engage Scripture in fresh ways, when a movement of the Spirit leads us to places we did not expect, we often find that beliefs we once held were arrived at second-hand, borrowed from people that we admire and respect. Borrowed convictions rarely stand the test of time and certainly do not nurture a deep relationship with Jesus.

I tell this story not to argue against Reformed theology. I still hold to many of its teachings and continue to be shaped and influenced by leaders from that tradition. I tell this story to show that we often uncritically hold to certain beliefs simply to belong to a community.

I am blessed with mentors and friends who encourage me to wrestle with Scripture. God has placed people in my life who have created a safe place for me to question and explore whatever God is doing in my heart at the time. A safe, loving community is an incubator for discerning one's convictions. Toxic, abusive communities demand conformity and encourage borrowed convictions.

In my work as a pastor I frequently encounter people who fiercely defend a conviction that they borrowed from someone else. I often find them to be tethered to hot-button or culture-war issues, like the age of the earth, the authority of Scripture, free will, what happens when we die, and so on. I encourage people to examine their beliefs from various angles by engaging with people and books that advocate views other than their own.

I have worked to make sure that the people under my care are free to (in good faith) examine and explore their convictions without fear of being removed from the communion of saints as expressed in our local church. When we experience a loving, Jesus-centered community, we are free to explore. We do not need to fear saying the wrong thing or being asked to leave if we don't align with the majority's beliefs (or, more likely, the convictions of the leader).

When we study the Scriptures, we start by asking questions. A lot of questions. We argue and wrestle with the Scriptures together and trust that the Spirit of the living God will guide us into understanding the truth in a way that each of us would discern and that we would openly and honestly share those convictions. As we engage in this process, we learn more about God, each other, and ourselves.

Toxic leaders thrive on borrowed convictions, demanding conformity from their followers. Critical questions are perceived as a threat to the community and the leaders that prop it up; thus, critical questions are disincentivized, if not outright forbidden. "We don't ask those questions here," or "Only heretics ask those kinds of questions" is the refrain of a toxic leader.

Followers of American Christian nationalism are incentivized to fall in line with the beliefs of the group. Questioning the beliefs of the group could signal that I am not part of the team and would likely put my belonging to the group at risk. In *How Minds Change* David McRaney calls this "tribal thinking." He notices that "Some ideas, the ones that identify us as members of a group, we don't reason as individuals; we reason as a member of a tribe. We want to seem trustworthy, and reputation management as a trustworthy individual often supersedes most other concerns."[20]

Members of a certain tribe, he continues, are willing to go to great lengths to show that they belong. In tribal environments, he argues,

> anything can become a signal of loyalty and how you signal will paint you as a good loyal member or a traitor. What you wear, the music you like, what car you drive, all of it. If an attitude or a belief or a stated opinion on an issue that was previously neutral becomes an identifier, it becomes a badge of loyalty or a symbol of shame, a signal to the others that you are not trustworthy.[21]

The borrowed convictions are not our own. They belong to the tribe and are cultivated by the tribal leaders.

Why do we believe the tribal leaders? McRaney argues, "We trust them because we identify with them. They share our values and our anxieties. They seem like us, or they seem like the people we would like to be. They share our attitudes, and so we are willing to share their beliefs."[22] We tend to trust people who say things we already agree with, especially if they believe that we share similar views of the world.

Many who hold to American Christian nationalist convictions do so because their tribal leaders tell them to, often with many reinforcing statements coming from within their community. As a borrowed conviction it will most likely change if they start following new leaders or commit to a new community.

AMERICAN CHRISTIAN NATIONALISM IGNORES MOST CHRISTIAN TRADITIONS

When American Christian nationalists argue that the United States should be a Christian nation, it is important to ask, "Which Christianity?" Consider the difference in convictions on the use of government power. Our Mennonite brothers and sisters are committed to nonviolence. If we have a Mennonite nation-state, will we absolve the Department of Defense and turn the Pentagon into a homeless shelter? Some of our Catholic brothers and sisters may argue for a nation-state in which the sanctity of life includes abolishing contraceptives and the death penalty. Our African American Methodist brothers and sisters may argue for government-funded reparations for slavery and Jim Crow laws. Is that what American Christian nationalists mean when they advocate for a Christian nation?

In my experience the answer to that is a resounding no! Those positions held by many Christians in America are deemed woke, socialist, and even evil. The Christianity that most American Christian nationalists argue for is a politically conservative, White, suburban version of Baptist, Reformed, Pentecostal, or nondenominational churches.

DOES RELIGIOUS NATIONALISM WORK? A BIBLICAL CASE STUDY

American Christian nationalists often appeal to the Old Testament as a foundational argument for their views. The argument goes something like this: "Look what God did with Israel; that is what he wants to do with America!"

This idea fails to come to grips with the actual history of ancient Israel, whose attempts at a type of religious nationalism failed to produce a God-honoring people (see Judges, 1–2 Chronicles, 1–2 Kings, and the prophetic literature).[a] These Scriptures tell the story of Israel, which was designed to be a theocracy (God is the ruler), elevating religious leaders (to greater or lesser degrees of piety and devotion) as the primary rulers. They had many religious policies that failed to produce a God-honoring society. In fact, many of the leaders were corrupt, and many of the religious policies were used to take advantage of the marginalized.

If the story of ancient Israel tells us anything, it is that religious government and laws do not produce God-honoring people in and of themselves. More often than not, these religious leaders become corrupted, distorting their witness of godliness and generating more evil in the world, under the guise of piety and holiness.

---

[a]Martin Sicker, *Judaism, Nationalism, and the Land of Israel* (New York: Routledge, 2019).

A WAY FORWARD

One of the earliest followers of Jesus was Saul of Tarsus, also called the apostle Paul. He was raised as a Jew under the Roman Empire. Before following Jesus he fought against Christians. After encountering the resurrected Jesus on the road to Damascus (Acts 9), he reordered his allegiances, reframed his identity, and lived the remainder of his life on a mission to share the good news of the kingdom of God with all the nations of the world (sometimes translated as "Gentiles").

To pursue his mission as an ambassador of the kingdom of God, Paul says that he strives to be "all things to all people" (1 Corinthians 9:19-23). You see this approach throughout Paul's life. Perhaps one of the most vivid is when he is facing an angry mob of his fellow Jews who were becoming violent toward him for preaching the gospel. Roman soldiers, charged with keeping the peace, escorted Paul to the local barracks. In the following texts, notice how Paul engages the different people according to their unique culture:

> As the soldiers were about to take Paul into the barracks, he asked the commander, "May I say something to you?"
>
> "Do you speak *Greek*?" he replied. "Aren't you the *Egyptian* who started a revolt and led four thousand terrorists out into the wilderness some time ago?"

Paul answered, "*I am a Jew*, from Tarsus in Cilicia, *a citizen of no ordinary city*. Please let me speak to the people."

After receiving the commander's permission, Paul stood on the steps and motioned to the crowd. When they were all silent, he said to them in *Aramaic* . . .

"*Brothers and fathers*, listen now to my defense."

When they heard him speak to them in *Aramaic*, they became very quiet.

Then Paul said: "*I am a Jew*, born in Tarsus of Cilicia, but brought up in this city. I studied under Gamaliel and was thoroughly trained in the law of our ancestors. I was just as zealous for God as any of you are today." (Acts 21:37-40; Acts 22:1-3, emphasis added)

Paul goes on to share that while he was persecuting followers of Jesus (he calls it "the Way"), he had a powerful encounter with Jesus, who called him to be an ambassador of reconciliation to all peoples. Paul says to the crowd,

Then the Lord said to me, "Go; I will send you far away to *the Gentiles*."

The crowd listened to Paul until he said this. Then they raised their voices and shouted, "Rid the earth of him! He's not fit to live!" (Acts 22:21-22, emphasis added)

As the murderous mob closed in on Paul, a Roman soldier stepped in and took him back to the barracks to figure out why they wanted to kill him. As part of their interrogation he had a soldier prepare a lash to get Paul to talk. Paul, knowing his rights as a Roman citizen, appealed to one of the soldiers and argued that it was not legal to torture a citizen of Rome apart from a trial:

The commander went to Paul and asked, "Tell me, are you a *Roman citizen*?"

"*Yes*, I am," he answered.

Then the commander said, "I had to pay a lot of money for my citizenship."

"But *I was born a citizen*," Paul replied. (Acts 22:27-28, emphasis added)

Notice how Paul identifies with "brothers and fathers" and honors his ethnic heritage (referencing the great Jewish teacher Gamaliel), while also subverting their claims to religious supremacy. When engaging the Roman soldiers, he speaks their language (Greek), identifies as a fellow citizen, and appeals to his legal rights as a Roman. All of this is in service of his ultimate allegiance, which is to Jesus, who he refers to as *Lord.*

Throughout Paul's ministry he engages in Jewish rituals, as well as holy days with his nation, even though many of them were not followers of the Way. He lives as a Jew and honors that way of being in the world. However, when these expressions of his ethnicity became a hindrance to the message of the kingdom of God, he set them aside (such as circumcision and food laws).

Paul also elevates the role of his government and appeals to his rights and privileges as a Roman (which many of his fellow Jews and Christians do not enjoy). However, he frequently criticizes Rome with the teachings and example of Jesus.

As a follower of the way of Jesus, Paul experiences and advocates for solidarity and communion with the transethnic, borderless (stateless) church, which is composed of many people who are neither Jewish nor Roman. The majority of his ministry is spent working to unite the various *nations* he encounters in Jesus. In summary,

► Paul is nationally or ethnically Jewish. He honors his Jewishness.

► Paul is civically Roman. He appeals to his Roman citizenship.

► Paul is ultimately a follower of Jesus and gives ultimate allegiance to him, all the while remaining a faithful member of the Jewish people and citizen of Rome.

Paul models for us a way of life that honors our relationship to the state, our ethnic identity, and our allegiance to Christ. Where American Christian nationalism works to conflate these three, Paul's example shows us a way forward.

POLITICAL CREATURES

In critiquing Christian nationalism I am not calling for a disengagement from politics. Far from it. Government is how we manage our common life together and is a space for us to love our neighbor as ourselves. American Christians within both parties can and should lead from their theological convictions, seeking to promote policies that they believe will cultivate human flourishing for all people. In this, we can model what it means to truly be a public servant.

While Christians often differ on how our theology should shape public policy, we can be united in practicing sacrificial love, generosity, and grace, especially when engaging with those aligned with the other party. However, we must remember that regardless of how many followers of Jesus serve in public office, the United States can never be more than a kingdom of this world. It will always fail to achieve that which only Jesus can accomplish: establishing the only true Christian society—the kingdom of God. While we wait for that day, we can engage in the political process while maintaining allegiance to Jesus and avoiding the temptation to give ourselves over to the kingdoms of this world. To tease out this principle, I'd like to share an illustration that has been helpful to me in understanding my engagement in the American political system.

I submit that there are five common attitudes toward politics that are less-than-ideal or downright harmful, and one that, though costly, is both wise and loving. I call the less-than-ideal postures the *partisans*, the *avoiders*, and the *warriors*. I'll illustrate these postures using select creatures.[23]

Partisans—elephant-donkey. Partisans give full allegiance to a political party. In modern America the two primary parties are represented by a donkey (Democrats) and an elephant (Republicans).

The *donkey* says it is progressive, committed to moving beyond the evils of our past. The *elephant* says it is conservative, committed to preserving the good things of our past.

While these views are not mutually exclusive, leaders in both parties often leverage the differences between the teams to create anxiety toward the other and garner more power.[24]

Occasionally, partisans may be true believers in their favored political ideology. However, the constantly shifting positions and beliefs in both modern parties show that often faithful partisans tend to go with the flow of their party leadership, maintaining allegiance to the elephant or donkey. As a result, they become tools of their party and enemies of the other.[25] By making the other team an enemy to fight, partisans often fail to love their neighbor as themselves.

Avoiders—ostrich-giraffe. Avoiders stay away from politics altogether. The *ostrich* hides its head in the sand instead of dealing with the messiness of managing our common life together. They may do so out of a sense of futility ("my vote doesn't matter") or because they view politics as inherently evil ("all politicians are corrupt").

The *giraffe*, like the ostrich, is disengaged from politics but for a different reason. The giraffe feels that they are above it all, often mocking the "meaningless quarreling" of the partisans and rolling their eyes at the warriors. Giraffes refuse to stoop down into the dirty business of politics. They believe it is beneath them.

Avoiders often fail to appreciate how politics affects their neighbors, especially those who are pushed to the margins. By disengaging from politics, avoiders fail to love their neighbor as themselves.

Warriors—dragon. Though warriors often disguise themselves in partisan garb, their methods reveal they are a different beast entirely, namely, the *dragon*. Whereas partisans focus on taking power in order to govern or advance specific policies, the dragon wants domination: power for the sake of power. They only advance policies if they believe doing so will give them more power.

Warriors are frustrated by the compromising partisans and the unengaged avoiders. They demand action saying, "We're in a war!" or "It is all or nothing!"

The primary goal of the *dragon* is not to advance policies but to dominate the culture, which often means the eviction or elimination of those who are not with them. As such, they fail to love their neighbors as themselves.

Those who take on these postures, while occasionally noble and thoughtful, usually fail to bring blessing, unity, and flourishing to the communities they are called to serve. Often, they cultivate pain, destruction, disunity, and sometimes violence and death. So what posture should followers of Jesus take? What posture best loves our neighbor as ourselves?

Servants—lamb. I submit that the wisest and most loving posture toward political engagement is that of the servant, as modeled by Jesus. Servants seek to use their power in service of others, seeking to bless, even at great cost to themselves (Matthew 20:28).

In what is possibly the most politically charged book of the Bible, Revelation, we see that the risen King Jesus is envisioned in a politically subversive way. Contrary to expectations, he is not imagined as a powerful bear or majestic eagle. To our surprise, the conquering King is primarily imaged as a slain-then-risen *lamb* (Revelation 5:9; John 1:29). The Lamb conquers the beastly evil powers not by military dominance or economic might but through self-sacrificing resurrection power. Followers of Jesus are called to live like him, the victorious Lamb, taking on the form of a servant (Philippians 2).

Jesus calls his followers to abstain from grasping for worldly power to leverage over others. That is what the kingdoms of this world do, and it leads to pain, destruction, and death. Jesus calls his followers to take the posture of the Lamb by leading with

- hospitality
- humility
- service
- longsuffering
- grace
- forgiveness
- selflessness
- and love (Matthew 20:25).

Jesus calls us to take up our cross and follow him, using his methods, taking his posture, and relying on his resurrection power as we engage in politics. While the posture of the Lamb seems weak and foolish (1 Corinthians 1:23) to *partisans*, *avoiders*, and *warriors*, it is ultimately by the power of the Lamb that we find redemption and restoration for the world.

5

DISARMING LEVIATHAN

Engaging Our Mission Field

Do you show contempt for the riches of his kindness,
forbearance, and patience, not recognizing that God's
kindness is intended to lead you to repentance?

ROMANS 2:4

AMERICAN CHRISTIAN NATIONALISTS PROVOKE FEAR, anxiety, and rage to grow their power and claim to meet our needs for safety, belonging, and purpose. But Leviathan always fails to deliver on its promises. It can only provide a pale facsimile of what is ultimately found in Jesus. So, what are we to do with the multitude caught in Leviathan's seductive grasp? We approach them as missionaries do, carrying the good news of the reconciling power of the gospel.

While Leviathan calls its followers to be culture warriors, Jesus calls his followers to be ministers of reconciliation. Warriors look to win the war by dominating and defeating the bad guys. Missionaries strive to be peacemakers, winning the hearts of their mission field through service, love, and restoration.

Restoration is the goal.

We work toward the gentle restoration (not defeat or destruction) of those we love who have turned away from Jesus toward Leviathan. We must take great care because many of those we wish to reach have internalized those deep feelings of fear, anxiety, and rage.

IN THE GRIP OF LEVIATHAN

How are we to reach those in Leviathan's grip? Before we attempt to engage our mission field, we must understand that the people we are trying to reach are not our enemies. The apostle Paul guides the way, saying,

> Finally, *be strong in the Lord and in his mighty power.* Put on the full armor of God, so that you can take your stand against the devil's schemes. *For our struggle is not against flesh and blood,* but against the rulers, against the authorities, against the powers of this dark world and against the spiritual forces of evil in the heavenly realms. (Ephesians 6:10-12, emphasis added)

Notice what he says: we are not in a fight with flesh and blood. We are not at war against these people. They are our mission field! These beloved image bearers of God are ensnared in the grip of a mighty, ancient, evil power that has been working since it distorted God's truth in the garden (Genesis 3), lobbied for Job's soul (Job 1), and will continue to work fighting the Lamb of God until the end (Revelation).

So, back to the initial question: How can we reach those caught in Leviathan's grasp? The same way we reach any people group with the gospel—we live as ambassadors, committed to consistent prayer, pursuing godly justice, proclaiming the gospel of peace, abiding in the truth of Jesus, and resting in his salvation by the strength of his Spirit.

Only by his power and work will those in our mission field truly find freedom. One day, the King of kings will ultimately defeat this ancient beast. Until that day comes, let us live like Jesus, working to reach those in Leviathan's grasp, calling them to believe in the good news that Jesus is the risen King.

Aunt Betty. Consider Aunt Betty. You probably know her or someone like her. You may well have a loved one that she reminds you of. Aunt Betty is, for the most part, a kind, earnest, patriotic, hardworking woman who loves Jesus, her family, and her country. For decades she has faithfully attended church services, Sunday school classes, and even the occasional revival when Billy Graham or his son Franklin would visit the nearest stadium.

Aunt Betty dutifully serves her community, hosting the check-in station at the Veterans Day parade, voting in every election, and even occasionally helping at the polling station. She organizes a group that places wreaths on the graves at the nearby veteran's cemetery on Memorial Day. She delights in anonymously paying for meals for those in uniform when she sees them dining at her favorite restaurant. She loves attending baseball games, watching fireworks on the Fourth of July, singing in the church choir, and visiting with friends on Sundays after the service. Aunt Betty has experienced the American civil religion and Christianity as an interwoven reality her whole life.

- ▶ Her hymnal houses "The Battle Hymn of the Republic" and "My Country 'Tis of Thee."
- ▶ She enjoys the red, white, and blue Bible cover she purchased at a Christian bookstore.
- ▶ Every day, she passes the "Faith, Family, Friends" sign from Hobby Lobby hanging near her front door.
- ▶ She appreciates the statement "In God We Trust" on her currency.
- ▶ Her nephew has a "Stand for the flag, kneel for the cross" sticker on his truck.
- ▶ She has heard patriotic sermons on the Sundays nearest Fourth of July, Veterans Day, and Memorial Day for most of her life.
- ▶ She has a commemorative plate on her wall with a picture of George Washington praying at Valley Forge.

For as long as she can remember, the conversations at her Sunday school class have tended to endorse conservative politics.

For Aunt Betty, singing the national anthem in the ballpark on Friday and singing "Amazing Grace" in church on Sunday is the same experience. Her civil religion is so interwoven with her Christian religion she does not distinguish between the two.

Aunt Betty's Christian nationalism is not a critically engaged, well-thought-out political philosophy. She did not wrestle through the Bible and the Constitution to discern this conviction. For her, Christian nationalism is a movement that encapsulates her religious and cultural values. It is an amalgamation of American civil religion and evangelical Christianity. In her thinking, the Christian nationalist platform promises to protect and promote her ethnic heritage and her faith.

Many of the American Christian nationalist leaders that Aunt Betty listens to sound like her pastor. They use words and phrases that come from Scripture, they frequently talk about God, and call us to pray for our country. They tell Aunt Betty that if we honor God, he will continue to bless America. If we do not, the consequences for our country will be devastating. She wants to glorify God and protect all that is beautiful in American culture, so she believes them when they tell her we must fight the culture war. If the "evil libs" take over, they will dishonor God, and our country will be lost. These leaders tell her that the devil is working in and through the "godless woke mob" who are trying to destroy our country. The steady flow of this rhetoric keeps Aunt Betty in a constant state of anxiety.

Like many others Aunt Betty is caught, ensnared by a movement that distorts the gospel of Jesus. Her political commitments and attitudes are formed by what is happening in her heart. And she is afraid of losing the things she holds dear.

How does Jesus call us to reach people like Aunt Betty? He does not call us to attack, shame, or belittle her. No, Jesus shows us that the best way to reach someone is by loving her like he does, seeking her restoration and healing.

We love like Jesus when we refuse to retaliate, assault, or treat Aunt Betty as an enemy to defeat. We love like Jesus when we see her and the multitude of others committed to American Christian nationalism as a mission field to reach. They are trapped, held captive by the lies of the evil one. Disentangling them from this ancient evil requires great care, precision, and love, like freeing a wounded deer from a barbed-wire fence.

The deer and the wire. Once while trekking through the forests of northern Arizona, I discovered the carcass of a deer that had become caught in a barbed-wire fence. The deer had struggled against the wire, yet the more it had wrestled, the more it had become entangled until it eventually died in this trap with no one to help. It was a gruesome sight.

I sometimes wonder what I would have done had I discovered this creature alive. What could I have done to free it?

First, I'd need to earn the animal's trust, approaching it gently and calmly, not reacting to its anxious response to my presence. I'd strive to bring a peace-filled, nonanxious presence and invite the deer to join me in the calm.

Second, I'd need to ensure my heart and mind were prepared to enter this delicate work. I may be wounded in the process of trying to free the captive. I need to prepare myself for the journey ahead. The degree to which the deer is tangled up in the wire will determine the time, energy, and patience this will require—I might be here for a while.

Third, I'd need the right tools. In this case, something like wire cutters may be in order. If I wasn't properly equipped, I'd likely create more frustration or, worse, harm.

Fourth, I'd need to use the tools correctly. This animal, full of anxiety and rage (and likely perceiving me as a threat), would be further damaged if I misapplied the tools. Not wanting to wound the one I wish to free, I need to practice using the tools to ensure I can apply them with a deft hand.

Finally, I'd need to provide care after the animal is freed. Being removed from the wire is a good starting point but certainly not the end. I must find others in my community who can apply healing. The longer the captivity, the deeper the wounds, and the greater the need for ongoing recovery.

I am often reminded of this story as I consider engaging with those whom Leviathan has claimed. It illustrates a guiding Scripture for this project: "Brothers and sisters, if someone is caught in a sin, you who live by the Spirit should restore that person gently. But watch yourselves or you also may be tempted. Carry each other's burdens, and in this way you will fulfill the law of Christ" (Galatians 6:1-2).

Those in Leviathan's grasp are fed a steady diet of fear, anxiety, and rage by various organizations. Like the deer in the wire, they are entangled, overtaken by evil. They will need to be restored with a calm spirit and carried gently.

The temptation will be to argue with Aunt Betty and to use facts, statistics, blog posts, and books to prove her wrong. But Aunt Betty is not giving her allegiance to Leviathan because it makes logical sense. She did not reason herself to this position. No, she has given allegiance to Leviathan because it promises safety, belonging, and purpose.

We approach Aunt Betty not as an enemy combatant but as a child of God whose allegiances are misplaced. And so we seek to be ministers of reconciliation.

As ministers of reconciliation our aim is not to defeat or destroy Christian nationalists, nor is it to dominate or abolish Leviathan (only Jesus can do that). We aim to restore our brothers and sisters with a gentle spirit, watching out for our souls so that we would not be tempted by arrogance, pride, apathy, or rage.

How do we do that? By the power of the Spirit, who produces in us love, joy, peace, patience, kindness, goodness, faithfulness, gentleness, and self-control (Galatians 5:22-23).

This same Spirit guides us to love in a way that

- ► is patient and kind
- ► is not jealous, boastful, proud, or rude
- ► does not demand its own way
- ► is not irritable
- ► does not keep a record of being wronged
- ► does not rejoice about injustice but rejoices whenever the truth wins out

▶ never gives up, never loses faith, is always hopeful, and endures through every circumstance (1 Corinthians 13:1-7).

As we love like Jesus, empowered by his Spirit, we can work to bring freedom to those caught in this great evil. As Galatians 6 says, our role is to seek to restore her gently, looking first at our hearts, lest we too be tempted. Then, with kindness, grace, love, and precision, we approach her, intending to point her back to Jesus and revive her to fellowship with him and with others.

THE ART OF TABLE SETTING (OR ON NOT FLIPPING TABLES)

I know that many of you who have picked up this book are, like me, angry about American Christian nationalism. You view it as a blight on the church. You hate it for what it's doing to your family, your friendships, and the country. You look at events like January 6, 2021, and want to yell, "This is wicked! Repent and believe the gospel!"

I get it. I hate Christian nationalism. I hate the damage it has done and is doing to people I love. I want to yell, pound the pulpit, and publicly denounce it as evil. I want to engage in the ministry of table flipping, like Jesus in the temple (see Matthew 21:12-13).

Frankly, there are times when it is wise and loving for some of us to do that. But while some are called to that prophetic ministry of *table flipping* (i.e., speaking God's truth, often to those in power), many more of us are called to reach the people who have been ensnared by Christian nationalism by engaging in the ministry of *table setting*.

In the marrow of my bones I believe in the prophetic role of the church, flipping tables when necessary. I am not calling us to give it up. I am calling us to follow the robust example of the ultimate prophet, Jesus, who set more tables than he flipped. When we engage as missionaries in the ministry of table setting, we practice humbly subversive, Holy Spirit–powered hospitality, remembering that the kindness of the Lord leads to repentance.

The majority of Jesus' mission work was done at tables. It has been said that Jesus ate his way through the Gospels.[1] At table fellowship he welcomed his enemies to become friends. He spoke heart-to-heart, in hospitality and love. He invites us to this approach today, to learn how humble subversion can lead to profound transformation.

It's time we learn how to set the table.

Does table setting work? Growing up, I frequently saw an ad campaign on television for the Hair Club for Men. At the end of the commercial a man with a thick head of hair would appear and boldly state, "I'm not just the president; I'm also a client." This was a catchy way to say, "I'm buying what I'm selling." The missionary method of table setting described in the following sections is not theoretical. I know that they genuinely work because they worked on me.

I was raised by good, loving parents in a politically and religiously conservative home. We went to church most Sundays, which I hated. The Jesus I perceived the church to be preaching was not someone I was interested in following. It seemed that many of these church folks didn't believe what they were saying. The words spoken on Sunday did not seem to have much impact on their behavior Monday through Saturday.

So, in my teens I gave up on church and became a neo-Nazi skinhead.

The core idea that bound our group together was that White people (especially those with blond hair and blue eyes) were superior to others and should lay claim to all forms of power to shape society and provide a safe future for White children.[2]

My commitment to this group did not start with an ideological conviction. It wasn't like I sat down one day with a textbook on genetics and reasoned my way to White supremacy. I was discipled into that way of thinking after I was welcomed into the community. I borrowed the tribe's convictions in order to belong.

Though the beliefs of White supremacy certainly appealed to my pride (I was born with blue eyes and blond hair, much of which has left me in recent years), it wasn't the belief that drew me in; it was what this group offered.

Being part of the crew gave me a community to belong to. They told me that I was part of something with a greater purpose (toxic as it was) and promised to watch my back when things got dangerous.

I was a fearful young man who longed for safety, belonging, and purpose, all three of which were offered by this brotherhood. After a few years I discovered that the promises of the group were empty. Neo-Nazi White supremacy could not deliver on its promises. I longed for the true safety and belonging of a community anchored in truth. What I experienced was empty rhetoric and broken promises. After a few years I left that group behind, mainly because I didn't see any wealthy, healthy, successful, retired skinheads. What they were preaching did not line up with what they were doing.

As a young man I was now lost, painfully longing for safety, belonging, and purpose. I was afraid I'd end up alone, without a community to belong to. To mask my fear I *raged*, expressing my feelings in combative statements and attitudes toward others. It made me feel powerful. If I was outraged, no one could hurt me. I raged about everything: politics, economics, the weather, religion, you name it.

Then, one day I was invited to play the drums at a church in North Phoenix. I remember thinking, *I should do some good stuff for God.* So, I agreed. Eventually, I joined the rotation of drummers, playing once or twice a month, then weekly.

I still didn't like church, but the people on the worship team were friendly, and it allowed me to play the drums frequently. After a while one of the guys in the band invited me to his house for dinner and beer. I thought to myself, *Beer? Christians don't do that!* So, I called his bluff and said yes. A few days later he and his wife welcomed me into their home, prepared a meal, and they really did have beers! We spent the evening eating, talking, and developing a friendship. They invited me back and eventually these meals became a weekly ritual.

One evening he said, "Why don't we talk about what makes you angry about Christianity." This was great! I had tons of material. He kindly sat and listened to my various expressions of rage, ranging from criticizing the hypocrisy of Christians I knew to the abuse of pastors and their failure to live out their sermons.

During these conversations, he'd often pause and say something like, "I share many of your concerns, and I think Jesus does too." Then he'd open a Bible and have me read parts of it. He asked what I thought Jesus thinks about our topic. I didn't know it, but he was discipling me and inviting me to follow the way of Jesus.

As time went on, I discovered that my mind and heart were changing. While I still resented hypocritical Christians, I liked Jesus and wanted to be part of what he was doing in the world.

That was more than twenty years ago. Eventually, I joined the staff of that church, went to seminary, got ordained, and now serve as the lead pastor. To my surprise Jesus even softened my heart toward those hypocritical Christians. I found that I had come to love the very people I had hated (though I am still very much a work in progress).

As I reflect on my experience, I see that God used the hospitality of a couple to create a safe space for me to process my thoughts and feelings. They also honored me by treating me as a friend, frequently inviting me into their home. By leading with questions, they invited me to share my perspective without fear of shame or embarrassment. They connected with my concerns, pointed to the good things I was saying, and then invited me to reconsider what Jesus might have to say about some of my misguided convictions and perspectives.

Consider the times when you have changed your mind about something. In what environment did you experience this change? It may be that you encountered a person or community that believed differently from you but was kind, hospitable, and gracious to you and created a safe space that allowed you to reexamine your convictions.

We usually do not change our minds because of someone's forceful argument or attack. My pastor, mentor, and friend, Rick, has said to me many times, "A person convinced against their will is of the same opinion still." Most people don't genuinely change by coercion, pressure, or force.

As missionaries we want to truly know the people we are seeking to serve by understanding what they believe, what they care about, and why they care. Truly knowing someone requires a genuine relationship built on hospitality, and so we work to set the table for relationships to grow. In the context of a safe community we can work to gently show the inconsistencies of their belief systems; by modeling what it looks like to live a Christ-centered life, we can show the beauty, joy, and power of the way of Jesus.

TRANSFORMATION STARTS IN THE HEART

Many of us have experienced a conversation with someone who passionately believes in a conspiracy theory they heard on talk radio or who is deeply anxious due to the influence of American Christian nationalist leaders. They may say some hurtful, harmful, and hateful things while expressing themselves. When faced with these types of conversations, there are usually three common reactions.

The first is to *ignore* the person and hope they stop talking about it.

The second is to *distance* ourselves from the person by asking them to leave or refusing to invite them to our gatherings again.

The third is to *argue* with the person, attempting to change their mind with better data.

However, these approaches rarely reshape someone's perspective. Instead, I suggest a fourth approach: *speak to the heart.*

Ignoring problems won't make them go away, distancing ourselves from others can lead to further entrenchment in their convictions, and arguing about facts rarely results in true change. Genuine transformation always starts with the heart. Communicating to the heart involves creating a hospitable space for others to share their fears and concerns and inviting them to explore their concerns with you. By engaging in this type of communication we can invite Jesus back into the conversation and pray for true transformation.

THE PYRAMID OF COMMUNICATION

Before we go any further, let's talk about the levels of conversations. There are many ways to think about the diverse types of communication we engage in. One of my favorites is what some call the pyramid of communication (see fig. 1).[3]

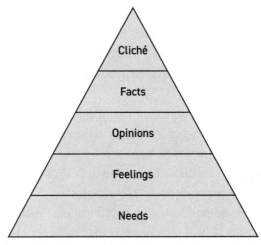

Figure 1. My interpretation of the five levels of communication

At the top of the pyramid are entry-level forms of communication, like clichés and facts. Exchanges at this level rarely reveal deep truths about who I am, my core convictions, or what I am genuinely passionate about.

In the middle of the pyramid are opinions, which are relatively safe ways to express something unique about us, but often do not involve much depth.

At the bottom are more profound forms of communication, such as feelings or, deeper still, our core needs.

At the top of the pyramid we have the kind of stuff that exists in the *head*. At the bottom of the pyramid we have conversations that express matters of the *heart*. As conversations move from the top to the bottom of the pyramid, we experience greater degrees of intimacy. At the same time, expressing matters of the heart means that we will experience increased vulnerability.

Clichés are commonly repeated phrases that are habitually spoken with little to no depth. Examples: "How are you doing today?" "What's up?" "Nice day we are having."

Facts include information about things outside of oneself, such as the weather, sports team statistics, or upcoming events. These rarely require vulnerability. Examples: "It's 100 degrees outside." "I am going to Argentina next week." "The score of the game is seven to three."

Opinions are concerns, dreams, desires, or expectations. When people give opinions, they share their perspectives, which can sometimes lead to conflict. Examples: "The Cowboys are not a good football team." "One hundred degrees is too dang hot." "Winter is the best time to visit Phoenix."

Feelings or emotions are heart-level communications. They are attempts to put words to what is going on in the core of our being (heart/soul). When we share our feelings, we are communicating heart-to-heart. Examples: "I am afraid I am going to fail." "I am so angry about the results of the recent election." "I feel alone."

Needs are the deepest level of communication. We usually communicate our needs only in relationships that we believe to be safe. Examples: "I am not safe in my relationship with my spouse." "I desperately need to belong somewhere."

Next time you are at a sports bar, listen to the conversations around you. Odds are most of them are at the top of the pyramid.

"How are you doing?" "Good. You?" (Cliché)

"The Cowboys are playing the 49ers today." "Dak Prescott has three fumbles this game." (Facts)

"The Cowboys were way better in the 1990s." (Opinion)

The people you are listening to are communicating. But they are communicating head-to-head, not heart-to-heart. They are not revealing their true selves to each other. The sports bar is likely not the best place for that anyway.

Let's leave the sports bar behind and move into the living room. Consider the best conversations you have had with friends and family. If you are anything like me, they are conversations centered on how you are feeling and how those feelings are connected to your core needs. These beautiful yet sometimes painful conversations are what we commonly refer to as heart-to-heart.

When engaging in conversations with our mission field, we have a choice to make—go head-to-head or heart-to-heart. We can spend our time arguing about facts and opinions. Or we can set those aside for the moment and humbly steer the conversation toward the heart.

Let's examine a conversation with Cousin Jim. While he may not be your actual cousin, many of us know about Cousin Jim. He's the guy at the family gathering, corporate party, or church small group who has said some things that seem crazy, hurtful, or even hateful, like "Some evil Jewish billionaire is funding thousands of drug-dealing rapists to invade our southern border to take our jobs!" Frankly, he can be a bit scary; he often gloats about his collection of assault rifles and recently shared that he purchased body armor for his family in the event of another civil war.

It can be tempting to engage Cousin Jim head-to-head. His statements don't line up with the facts. He is wrong and in need of correction. However, his head will only change once he experiences a change of heart.

Instead of arguing with him, we can invite him to a deeper level of connection. We can invite him into a heart-to-heart conversation. We could respond with something like: "Tell me why this is important to you." (Notice we are not agreeing with him.)

As you listen, remember that the things he is saying (facts and opinions) are tied to what he is feeling. In this case it is likely *fear*. In this scenario we could attempt to connect heart-to-heart by saying something like, "Jim, when I hear that statement, I feel fear in my chest," or "When I hear that, my heart skips a beat." Then, invite Cousin Jim to share. "What do you feel when you hear that?"

Now that we have connected with the feeling, we can work to foster safety in the conversation by finding a point of agreement. Perhaps something like this: "I love that you care deeply about this issue. I do too. I agree with you that our government should provide safety at our borders. I long for a safe community here in [your city] to raise families, work, and live."

Then, we can engage in humble subversion by reintroducing Jesus to the conversation: "Lately, I've been thinking about what the Bible says about caring for immigrants. I think about the people running for their lives and wonder if Jesus might be calling me to care for them in some way. It is something I feel conflicted about. How do we hold these two things together—safety for our community and care for the immigrant?"

Finally, we can show honor and dignity to our conversation partner by asking for Cousin Jim's perspective: "What do you think Jesus might have us do for immigrants seeking safety and peace?"

The conversation started with something that sounded crazy or bigoted. This statement likely came from a place of anxiety or rage. Instead of ignoring, dismissing, or rejecting the conversation, we engaged by asking more questions and steering the conversation from *head* to *heart*. This hopefully had the effect of creating a safe space for our conversation partner to talk about and process their currently held beliefs and share their perspective.

Engaging in heart-to-heart conversations with American Christian nationalists has the added benefit of communicating that we are a safe conversation partner ready to talk about these things whenever they are, without fear of excluding them from our community.

CHANGING YOUR MIND IS SCARY AND COSTLY: THE NEED FOR THE LOCAL CHURCH

The process of repentance can feel like a dangerous undertaking. It often costs us something. Changing our minds could mean no longer being accepted by a group of friends or an organization. A change of conviction may lead to the death of relationships. This is scary.

Those experiencing a change of mind and heart need the safety and peace of belonging to a trusted community. This is where the local church comes in. The local church is bound together not by common opinions, political convictions, ethnicity, or socioeconomic status. The local church is bound together by Jesus, who welcomes everyone to his table.

The people currently committed to American Christian nationalism need hospitable, loving church communities that allow them to ask questions, process their thoughts and feelings, and share their perspectives without fear of being excluded.

Depending on your church tradition, this could be a small group, a Sunday school class, a weekday program, or an evening potluck. How can your church community create a safe, hospitable space for American Christian nationalists in your community to experience healthy transformation, confession, repentance, and reconciliation?

CULTIVATING MISSIONAL CONVERSATIONS

In the remainder of this chapter we will look at seven practices and principles for healthy missional conversations. These elements are designed to cultivate healthy, Jesus-centered discussions with the people in our mission field and are crucial when speaking about controversial or politically charged topics.

1. Start with hospitality. Our minds change when our hearts feel safe, which can be cultivated through the spiritual discipline of hospitality. Consider the example of Jesus, who frequently dined with others. A quick survey of the Gospels reveals that Jesus ate with all sorts of people, and, for the most part, they felt welcome with him at the table.

When we show hospitality, we communicate that the person we have invited to our table is welcome, seen, respected as an image-bearer of God, and loved by us. As Theodore Roosevelt supposedly said, "Nobody cares how much you know until they know how much you care." Most of us are not interested in listening to someone who doesn't value us. True hospitality is a powerful way to show that we care and to earn the right to be heard.

One of my favorite ministries in Phoenix is Young Life. This organization seeks to reach teenagers with the good news of Jesus through deep, loving relationships and a lot of fun! I have been honored to participate in a few Young Life gatherings and camps over the years and have seen the power of hospitality at work. I have witnessed Young Life leaders close out Barro's Pizza, having four-hour conversations with two teens about faith, football, and Fortnight. I have watched PhD candidates play air guitar to Blink 182 in a living room full of twenty-five sweaty, smelly teens. These individuals are earning the right to be heard.

The Settlers of Catan tournaments, camp fundraisers, and late-night runs to Sonic are all expressions of hospitality. They are meeting the students in their context—speaking their language, eating their favorite food, and experiencing the music they enjoy. Young Life leaders are excellent at ministering in places that their mission field is comfortable in. Like Jesus, they go where the people are.

In Young Life this means spending time at fast-food joints, buying diapers for teen moms, spending a week at summer camp, and showing up at high school football games. What does hospitality look like for American Christian nationalists? What restaurants could you take them to or what gatherings could you prepare that would help earn the right to be heard? At what events could you join them? This could be visiting the Veterans Cemetery on Memorial Day with them, sharing biscuits and gravy at Cracker Barrel, or inviting them over for a Fourth of July cookout.

One missionary I spoke with worked with an organization that sought to reach the Islamic community. Their mission statement was "With love and respect, inviting all Muslims to follow Jesus." He shared that the missionaries who were part of this organization lived in such a way that their mission field knew they cared about them.

When a child was sick in the community, they knew they could call the missionary because they cared. There were even occasions when they would ask the missionary to pray for the sick. While they didn't share the same beliefs, they knew the missionary loved them.

As you strive to reach American Christian nationalists, I invite you to look for opportunities to serve them, love them, shower them with compassion, and pray for them. Showing hospitality may feel counterintuitive, but remember that the way of Jesus is radically different from the ways of this world.

Hospitality and safety. American Christian nationalism provides a toxic form of community by stirring anxiety and promising to meet our core need to belong. True belonging means that I can share what is happening inside of me (my concerns, thoughts, fears, and needs) without fear of expulsion. American Christian nationalist organizations do not provide true belonging. They do not encourage or allow questions critical of their position, posture, or the integrity of their leaders. If you ask the wrong question, you will be chastised and possibly expelled, labeled as a betrayer (e.g., RINO or closet Marxist).

Our mission field needs Jesus-centered communities to belong to while they process their questions. They need to know that as long as they are present and operating in good faith (e.g., not attacking other people), they are welcome to be their true selves with us.

Hospitality communicates "You are welcome here." When a person is ready to leave American Christian nationalism, they need a place to land, a genuine community of safe, loving people.

Consider Aunt Betty. After months of conversation with you, she reads in her American flag–covered Bible a portion of Scripture that talks about caring for immigrants. This thought haunts her and she begins to wonder, *What if my attitude toward immigrants is not what Jesus wants from me?*

Now, standing at the kitchen sink, looking out the window while Christian nationalist media is blaring from the TV in the living room, she begins to feel conflicted between the rhetoric of her leaders and the Scripture she has been reading.

At that moment, who can she call?

Is there someone she will feel safe to process these thoughts and feelings with?

She worries that if she brings up her concerns with her fellow American Christian nationalists she will be viewed as a threat. Maybe they'll say she has flip-flopped or gone woke, and she'll be kicked out of the group.

Leviathan promises belonging, but it never truly delivers. She needs a hospitable place that will welcome her in the process of renewing her mind.

My friend Randy has served all over the world as a missionary with Food for the Hungry and Vision of Community Fellowship. During one of our conversations, we talked about the methods Jesus used when ministering to the people he encountered. He shared that Jesus' approach to ministry was anything but formulaic. He used many different approaches with people based on their context and circumstances, but Jesus constantly invited them to have a relationship with him. Jesus' approach was marked by radical hospitality. He was always welcoming others into heart-to-heart conversations. As we approach American Christian nationalists, let us strive to be like Jesus and lead with hospitality.

Put it into practice. Heart-to-heart conversations are best in the context of hospitality. Make a list of opportunities where you can show grace, kindness, and hospitality to your mission field.

2. Lead with questions. Good-faith questions are an invitation to engage at a deeper level. When we approach people with curiosity, we set the table for heart-to-heart communication and invite them to discern their own convictions. In their book *Arguing Like Jesus*, Joe Carter and John Coleman write, "By asking your listeners something rather than preaching to them or giving them answers, you let them come to their own conclusions, which often forces them to be more emotionally and intellectually attached to those conclusions."[4] When we lead with statements instead of asking questions, we run the risk of disengaging from heart-to-heart conversation.

If we become argumentative, we may signal that we are not a safe person to process new ideas. Regardless of the topic of conversation, healthy missionaries strive to create hospitable environments by following the example set by James, the brother of Jesus, who said, "Everyone should be quick to listen, slow to speak and slow to become angry, because human anger does not produce the righteousness that God desires" (James 1:19-20).

Quick to listen, slow to speak. For those of us who love to argue, this is a bummer of a text. One of my prevailing sins is to briefly listen to someone and then jump in with an argument, seeking to win the debate. This is being quick to speak. But as James notes, cutting people off in a conversation is not loving; leading with questions and listening with the goal of understanding is.

A discipline I have found helpful is tracking the amount of time I spend talking and listening during a conversation. As a rule of thumb I strive to spend twenty minutes listening for every ten minutes talking. Another helpful tactic is to ask my conversation partner if I can repeat what I understand them to be saying. If I am not able to articulate their position in a way that they wholeheartedly agree with, I have not truly understood. I need to ask more questions and seek to actively listen.

Put it into practice. Create a list of go-to questions to use in conversations with your mission field. This could include open-ended questions like, "Tell me what you mean by that," "I'd like to hear you talk more about that," or "Tell me why that is important to you."

3. Connecting on shared values. During one of his missionary journeys the apostle Paul visited the Greek city of Athens. He desired to introduce them to Jesus, and he worked to find ways to connect with them. As he walked around the city, he observed that there was an idol to an unknown god (Acts 17:23). Paul recognized that he and the Athenians shared the value of spirituality and truth-seeking. He leveraged these shared values to connect with the Athenians and talk about Jesus.

As Carter and Coleman say, "A method for stirring the hearts of your audience is to utilize shared or common values. As human beings, some concepts inherently move us, and some ethical imperatives compel us to action."[5] By connecting with the values of our mission field, we can show that a new idea fits within the framework of what they already believe.

As missionaries desiring to connect on shared values, we first must know our own values! In the book *Saving Us*, Katharine Hayhoe encourages us to take an inventory of our story, our values, and our heroes, and to use them as anchors for heart-to-heart conversation. She invites us to "figure out where to open a discussion, take inventory of who you are and what you might have in common with others you know and meet."[6] This inventory could include beliefs that we value, traditions, people or possessions that we hold dear, events that we celebrate, hobbies we pursue, and even the idols we are tempted to worship.

Put it into practice. Do a values inventory. (1) Write down your values, those things that are deeply important to you and that you strive to embody in your life. (2) Write down what you believe the core values of American Christian nationalists are. (3) Pray that God will show you items that connect between the two lists.

Do some research. (1) Visit the restaurants, grocery stores, and community centers that your mission field frequents. Notice the signage, listen to the conversations, observe people's clothing, the cars they drive, and the bumper stickers they display. (2) Check out the TV shows they watch, their favorite radio stations, and their social media outlets. What concerns, values, and dreams do these things reveal?

4. I am not your enemy: red flags and shibboleths. Two of my heroes of the faith who are also my friends, have ministered to a community in Afghanistan for two decades. For safety reasons I am changing their names to Chris and Erin. Most of their ministry has taken place during America's war with Al-Qaeda. Could you imagine being a missionary to a people that your home country is at war with? That is a tough assignment.

During one of our conversations, Chris shared that one of the greatest challenges they face is convincing people that they are not an enemy.

While Chris and Erin do not agree with many of the religious and political beliefs of their Afghan neighbors, they work diligently to develop healthy relationships by showing radical love and hospitality and seeking to honor as much of their host culture as possible. Once the people of their mission field recognized that Chris and Erin were for them, they were open to heart-to-heart conversations. Friendships developed, and Jesus was introduced in safe, healthy, and gracious ways.

As I was talking with Chris about the aim of this book to equip people to reach American Christian nationalists, he said something encouraging. "You have an awesome opportunity because you are already so close to your mission field! You wear the same clothes, you listen to the same music, you eat the same food, and you have established family ties and friendships with the people you hope to reach. Moreover, you look and talk like your mission field."

Chris is right. God has blessed us with many ways to connect and communicate that we are not an enemy. I know that it may seem like American Christian nationalists are the bad guys. While the ideology is certainly destructive, the people who are given over to it are our mission field and likely include people that you love and have a relationship with. As a missionary this is good news! Half the work is done. God has placed you in their lives and given you a beautiful opportunity to reach them with the life-giving hope of the good news of Jesus!

This is especially helpful because many of them do feel surrounded by enemies. They sense that they are constantly being pushed around and bullied. They feel estranged from the communities they grew up in. The world they thought they knew is becoming stranger and more dangerous by the day. They believe they are losing their culture to an invading enemy. Psychologist Dave Verhaagen argues that this posture toward others can sometimes be attributed to *hostile attribution bias*, noting:

> Christian nationalists are not only harsh and critical toward others, but they see others as hostile toward them, even when the evidence does not suggest it. Christian nationalists appear to be prone to hostile attribution bias, which means they see others as having hostile intentions, even where none exist. Their mental filter makes them see others as intending them harm and ready to pounce.[7]

Given that many in our mission field are more likely to see anyone who questions their movement as enemies, we should be watchful of ways we may accidentally communicate that we are the opposition.

Let us consider our posture. When those in our mission field share their current beliefs or opinions, how do we behave toward them? If our hearers feel attacked, belittled, or shamed, they will either power up or shut down. David McRaney notes, "If they believe that your position is that they are gullible or stupid or deluded or in the wrong group or a bad person, then of course they will resist, and the facts will now be irrelevant."[8] We need to consider if we are being hostile, argumentative, or dismissive. We should avoid statements and attitudes that communicate "I am not safe."

Shibboleths and red flags. A *shibboleth* is a word or phrase that distinguishes insiders from outsiders. Like a code or password, a shibboleth is a way to identify yourself as an ally. Failing to properly present a shibboleth can signal that you are an outsider or worse, an enemy.

The term comes from the book of Judges, which describes a military conflict between the Gileadites and the Ephraimites.

> The Gileadites captured the fords of the Jordan leading to Ephraim. Whenever a fugitive from Ephraim said, "Let me cross over," the men of Gilead asked him, "Are you an Ephraimite?" If he replied, "No," they said, "All right, say 'Shibboleth.'" If he said, "Sibboleth," because he could not pronounce the word correctly, they seized him and killed him at the fords of the Jordan. (Judges 12:5-6)

The word, which originally meant "ear of grain," was difficult for Ephraimites to pronounce, and so *shibboleth* was used by the Gileadites to discern between friend and foe. By saying the word correctly, a person signaled that they were safe. What are phrases or statements that would communicate "I am one of you"? Consider how the following statements might serve as shibboleths when reaching out to American Christian nationalists.

- ► We need safe borders.
- ► God bless America!
- ► I love my country.
- ► I also have concerns about the direction of our country.
- ► I don't think America needs to shift left or right, we need to look up!

A form of shibboleth could also include activities such as sharing stories of what you love about America, flying an American flag during patriotic holidays, posting a positive quote from one of America's founders on social media, or praying that God would bless America at the next social gathering.

The opposite of a shibboleth is a *red flag*, a word or phrase that communicates "I am your enemy." Words or phrases like *social justice, woke, systemic injustice, corporate repentance, Democrats make some good* points, *January 6 was an insurrection,* or *I watched MSNBC last night* could unintentionally communicate "I am not safe."

As missionaries we want to use shibboleths and avoid red flags in conversations with our mission field so we might build trust and show ourselves to be safe conversation partners.

IF YOU DO USE RED FLAGS, BE QUICK TO DEFINE THEM

As a pastor I frequently use the term *social justice* because I believe it clarifies the concepts of justice and righteousness in Scripture. The gleaning in Ruth, the Jubilee in Leviticus, and so on are not interpersonal, criminal, or environmental justice. They are practices of justice between groups of people (landowners and those who had to sell their land, those with fields, and those without food); they are *social* forms of justice.

The early church practiced social justice (Acts 2:42-46; Acts 5; Acts 6), and it's what Paul appeals to in his fundraising for those in Jerusalem experiencing famine (1 Corinthians 9-11).

However, using the phrase will likely signal a red flag to some of my hearers. To signal that I am not an enemy, I quickly define it by addressing the fact that some folks in the media are using the phrase differently from what I mean. It is a term used by theologians for over one hundred years, including trusted figures like John Stott and Carl Henry.

Put it into practice.

► Red flags. Consider the values, dreams, and taboos of your mission field. Write out a list of words or phrases that might communicate that you are not a safe conversation partner. Work to avoid using these in future conversations.

► Shibboleths. Thinking again of the values, dreams, and taboos of your mission field, write a list of words or phrases that communicate "I am a safe conversation partner." The best phrases are ones that connect to shared values.

5. Honor the good. I have researched American Christian nationalism in a variety of settings, and my absolute favorite spot is an independently owned café down the road from where I live. There are many similar eateries across the country, and while each is unique, they share a lot in common. It is a category of restaurant that I call "Downhome Café."

These are mom-and-pop restaurants with an eclectic mix of 1950s nostalgia and red, white, and blue decor accompanied by a smattering of "Faith-Family-Friends" signs from Hobby Lobby.

On the menu? A killer chicken-fried steak that will make you lose your religion, and a never-ending cup of coffee that tastes like it was brewed seventeen years ago in an industrial plant outside Duluth.

Perhaps you have a Downhome Café where you live. Maybe you've been there recently. If not, I invite you to visit soon. It is a great spot to learn about our mission field. When you visit, you'll probably experience something like the following observations.

As you take your seat for breakfast, you look around and notice the hardworking men and women who feel at home in this space.

At the table next to you, you overhear an aging patron boast to the effervescent waitress about his adult son's award for Spanish-speaking newscaster of the year.

In the corner, a table of eight Army veterans swap stories of adventure and bravery from their time as teenagers fighting in Vietnam.

A few tables over three Latino farm workers are talking with a man with a belt buckle the size of your head at an adjacent table about their plans for the upcoming holiday.

Over at the big table is a multigenerational family celebrating the six-year-old's birthday over pancakes.

Near the back is a crew from a local manufacturing plant debating the best method for tuning the carburetor of a 1978 Ford Bronco.

As you admire the multitude of crosses and faith-based signs adorning the wall flanking pictures of James Dean and Frank Sinatra, Jeanette, your server, comes up to take your order.

"What'll ya have, hun?"

Okay, freeze! Take a moment to process this scene as a missionary. Examine the cultural values, traditions, taboos, and dreams represented in this room. There is beauty and good here if we have eyes to see it.

The apostle Paul calls us to this posture, saying, "Finally, brothers and sisters, whatever is true, whatever is noble, whatever is right, whatever is pure, whatever is lovely, whatever is admirable—if anything is excellent or praiseworthy—think about such things" (Philippians 4:8).

What are some of the things about this culture that you can celebrate? As we interact with our mission field, let us strive to honor the good.

What are the good, praiseworthy things about our mission field that we can dwell on? Perhaps it would be the value of hard work, the deep love of country, a willingness to sacrifice for each other, a strong love of neighbor, deep family ties, and a profound love of the land they live on (I'm looking at you, Wendell Berry), working with your hands, contentment, and frugality (fixing things instead of just buying something new).

Though it might seem easy to dismiss, shame, or belittle American Christian nationalists, we must remember that they are fellow children of God with inherent dignity and worth. C. S. Lewis illustrates this, saying, "There are no ordinary people. You have never talked to a mere mortal. . . . [I]t is immortals whom we joke with, work with, marry, snub and exploit."[9]

No ordinary people. Wow. Lewis is (as usual) right on. The people we are working to reach are just that—people. They are not monsters to destroy or enemies to slay. They are people made in the image and likeness of God (Genesis 1:26), worthy of our dignity and respect. While we must strive to not be perceived as enemies, we must, more importantly, guard our hearts to ensure that we do not see them as our enemies.

Theologian Maria Cimperman shares the story of a brave Christian leader who worked to reach the infamous terrorist Joseph Kony with the good news of Jesus. She writes,

Peacebuilding and work toward reconciliation, for example, require great hope. A story is told about Archbishop John Baptist Odama serving in northern Uganda, the region where the Lord's

Resistance Army was primarily located. He regularly went into the camps of Joseph Kony, leader of the notorious group, and even spent the night there. When people asked why he did this (he could be killed), he simply answered, "Joseph is a child of God. He is one of my sheep, too."[10]

Each person we seek to reach is worthy of honor and dignity. Some may be concerned that showing honor to an American Christian nationalist would be perceived as approval of the bad stuff in their life. As missionaries we must remember that when we honor the good, we are not endorsing the bad.

Honoring the good is not endorsing the bad. Both of my grandfathers served in the Pacific during WWII. I am enormously proud of their service and I share their stories with my children. I celebrate their desire to serve our country. I praise them for putting their lives in harm's way for the sake of America and others. I honor their courage, patriotism, and bravery.

Both of my grandfathers also had their failures and flaws. Some I witnessed; others I have only heard in stories. I share some of those flaws and failures with my children, not to shame my grandfathers but to help my children understand that we come from a people prone to certain expressions of evil, and by being aware of them we can work to do better in our lifetime.

My wife is Sicilian. Her parents bravely immigrated to Brooklyn in the 1970s. Both of her grandfathers also fought in the war, on the other team. Both men, being patriotic Italians, fought for the fascist dictator Benito Mussolini.

We also share their stories with my children. Sharing the honorable things as examples to follow and dishonorable things as examples to avoid. By telling my children stories of their great-grandfathers, we hope to pass on what is good and to learn to repent (turn away) from that which is dishonorable.

Honoring the good in a person is not tacit approval or endorsement of the bad.

We find this principle throughout Scripture. Take King David for example. He is referred to as a "man after [God's] own heart" (1 Samuel 13:14). He had some great moments of faith, courage, and generosity. He also had some really bad moments of cowardice, faithlessness, rape, and murder.

When we meditate on David's psalms, we are not endorsing his evil behavior. In wisdom we are also not whitewashing the sinful acts that he committed. As students of Scripture we gain wisdom from the good and the bad, understanding David holistically, as a real person. The Scripture tells us that people are not totally good or totally bad but, as Russian author Aleksandr Solzhenitsyn said, "If only there were evil people somewhere insidiously committing evil deeds, and it were necessary only to separate them from the rest of us and destroy them. But the line dividing good and evil cuts through the heart of every human being."[11]

American Christian nationalists value many honorable things. Love of country. Honoring those who put their life on the line in service of one's country. Hard work and industriousness. The value of family and the unborn child. A recognition of God and a desire to honor him. The dignity of people who work the earth. The responsibility of parents to guide and raise their children. The value of the church to the community. Public expressions of patriotism and shared civic values of life and liberty.

It can sometimes be easy to focus on the bad in our mission field, treating American Christian nationalists as one-dimensional monsters, even casting shame and derision on them. We may find ourselves hating them. When this happens, we are no longer taking on the posture of a missionary. *A person who hates the culture of their mission field is not a missionary but a colonizer.*

A good missionary shares the good news of Jesus with people expecting they will live it out in a way that is authentic to their culture. A colonizer expects them to receive their version of the gospel *and* to live it out in ways that align with the colonizer's culture.

I have fallen for this temptation multiple times, often finding myself feeling judgmental not only of the nationalistic ideology being propagated but also of the culture of those who hold to it. I often rolled my eyes and silently mocked some of their cultural expressions. I found myself wanting them to stop being them and start being like me. *I had become a colonizer*, working to force my cultural preferences onto them. I not only wanted them to follow Jesus but also to stop eating at Cracker Barrel.

By seeking to honor the good of our mission field, we can protect ourselves from taking the attitude of a colonizer. As missionaries we can work to celebrate, dignify, and honor the culture of our mission field and then work to introduce them to Jesus with the expectation that they will follow him in a unique way that aligns with their culture. Good missionaries want to see people in all cultures follow Jesus and worship him in their own way.

Put it into practice. First, seek to discover the good among Christian nationalists. Second, as you observe your mission field, create a list of the core values you believe are underneath their stories, taboos, and rituals. This could include things like a strong work ethic, love, commitment to neighbors, and the like.

6. Humble subversion. The postures previously listed work together to cultivate a hospitable environment for our mission field to feel welcome and safe to engage in heart-to-heart conversation. At this point in the process we can engage in humble subversion by asking honest, guided questions that work to disrupt their presently held beliefs and point back to Jesus. I include several examples in chapter seven.

Many American Christian nationalists hold to *borrowed convictions* that their tribal leaders pressure them to believe. Many of these convictions are incongruent with the teachings of Jesus. By asking guided questions and pointing back to Jesus, we sow seeds of change in the garden of their minds that may one day bear the fruit of repentance.

Just as with actual seeds, the fruit comes through patient, gentle cultivation. The amount of humbly subversive conversations needed for true change is different for each person. There is no quick fix. I say this both to encourage you and to set expectations. Rarely does someone change their mind in the context of a single conversation. It usually involves multiple meetings, time to reflect, and space to wrestle through their ideas. And, as with many actual seeds, there may be no root or fruit at all.

Put it into practice. Consider the values, fears, taboos, stories, and hopes of your mission field. What are some humbly subversive questions you can ask that would show how Jesus ultimately fulfills these longings? Write a list (I give some examples in chapter 7) and consider ways that you can address them the next time they come up in conversation.

7. Open invitation to future conversation. As a final step in any missionary encounter, remember to cultivate hospitality, always leaving an open invitation to continue the conversation. We want to explore the deep, heart-level needs and fears of our mission field and reintroduce them to Jesus, not win a debate. Sometimes our conversation partners may feel vulnerable and afraid. Exposing heart-level needs and fears can leave someone open to betrayal, mockery, toxic shame, and abandonment.

As we end our conversations, we want to build trust, safety, and hospitality by inviting them to continue the conversation in the future and to let them know that regardless of the disagreements, you are committed to staying in the relationship for their good.

Put it into practice. Heart-to-heart conversations take time—a *lot* of time. Review your calendar and schedule times to invest in your mission field. Consider inviting them to join you in something structured, like a weekly Bible study or monthly prayer meetings. Perhaps you could create your own recurring event, like a walk in the park, card game, or meal.

FOUR COMMITMENTS FOR HEALTHY CONVERSATIONS

Like you, I have engaged in many difficult conversations with people that I disagree with. My counselor, Phil, says that there are some key commitments that I need to have before engaging in difficult conversations. I have modified his work for our purposes and presented them as four commitments for healthy conversations with our mission field. These four commitments encapsulate the seven steps outlined in this chapter.

Patience. I commit to being patient as they unwind whatever is going on inside of them.

Perception. I commit to striving to perceive what is going on inside of my heart during the conversation.

Powerlessness. I commit to recognizing my powerlessness to change their beliefs. That is the work of the Holy Spirit.

Invitation. I commit to inviting them into deeper conversations and relationships (if it is healthy to do so).

I invite you to pray through these commitments before difficult meetings. I have found that they soften my heart and remind me to set healthy boundaries and expectations for myself.

6

MEETING LEVIATHAN

Preparing Our Hearts for the Work

The news about him spread all the more, so that crowds of
people came to hear him and to be healed of their sicknesses.
But Jesus often withdrew to lonely places and prayed.

LUKE 5:15-16

MANY OF US HAVE BEEN THERE: hanging out at a family gathering when someone shares something they read in a chain email or heard at a political rally. As they talk, their voice gets louder and begins to crack. You can tell they are passionate about the issue and are convinced of the veracity of their claims.

You think what they are saying sounds like clickbait, hate speech, or a conspiracy theory. You begin to wonder how to respond. As you plan your next move, you notice that you are experiencing strong feelings. It may be anger, fear, disgust, shame, or a mixture of all four. The temptation to yell, ignore, or run away begins to cloud your mind. It feels overwhelming.

Whether it's a work party, church gathering, Christmas dinner, Fourth of July cookout, or Aunt Betty's birthday, we can show love to those we hope to reach by investing time in preparing our hearts for the work. Like a missionary entering a foreign culture, we can intentionally connect with Jesus, check in with our hearts, rest, frame the opportunity, pray for those we hope to engage, and even invite a team of supporters to pray for us during the gathering.

START WITH WHY

A while back I was talking with a pastor friend who shared that he was exasperated with American Christian nationalists and felt anger at the destructive nature of the movement. After I shared my vision for this book, he asked, "What makes you even want to do this?"

This was the first time I remember someone asking me *why* I wanted to reach American Christian nationalists. My answer was that I love them. Not in a general way—I love them because they are my community, my church, my family, my people. They are me.

When I feel helpless and afraid, I am, like them, tempted to wield the sword of worldly power to protect me and mine.

As a follower of Jesus I know that grasping for worldly power will ultimately lead to despair, destruction, and death. Out of love I want them to discover or return to the way of Jesus, which is the same thing I want for myself when I stray.

What about you? How would you answer my pastor-buddy's question? Why do you want to reach American Christian nationalists? What is your *why*? If the reason is love, being reminded of this can cultivate compassion and empathy in your soul.

I want to ask you a question that will require the use of your Spirit-led imagination. I'd like you to imagine someone in your mission field: maybe a family member, friend, coworker, neighbor, or perhaps someone in your church. Once you have them in mind, I invite you to consider how you'd answer this question: How would their life be different if they experienced Jesus-centered repentance and restoration?

I know that idea may seem impossible. It may seem that they are in too deep or are too far gone, but what if God did a transformative work in their life? Can you imagine it?

God has done mighty works of restoration before. Consider Saul of Tarsus. In Acts 8 Saul is described as someone who worked to destroy the church. The next chapter describes Saul's encounter with the risen Jesus, which brings him to repentance. During this encounter, Saul becomes blind.

Jesus then appeared to a man named Ananias and called him to work toward Saul's restoration. He called Ananias to go and "ask for a man from Tarsus named Saul. . . . [He is waiting for you to place your] hands on him to restore his sight" (Acts 9:11-12).

Ananias, skeptical of Saul's conversion, pleaded with the Lord, "I have heard many reports about this man and all the harm he has done to your holy people in Jerusalem. And he has come here with authority from the chief priests to arrest all who call on your name" (Acts 9:13-14).

Ananias rightly recognized the harm Saul had done to the followers of Jesus. He was a dangerous person! And yet Jesus responded to Ananias, "Go! This man is my chosen instrument to proclaim my name to Gentiles and their kings and to the people of Israel" (Acts 9:15).

Jesus called Ananias to heal someone who had actively sought to destroy the church. What do you think Ananias felt when he heard God call him to seek the restoration of someone who was engaged in violence against his people? The text does not tell us. But Ananias was so convinced in the redemptive power of the risen Jesus that he obeyed God and sought to bring healing to someone who had once claimed to be his enemy. Saul experienced a redemption far beyond all expectations.

I invite you to spend time prayerfully dreaming about a hope-filled future for your Christian nationalist neighbors. How might the redemptive work of Jesus transform their lives? What would their lives be like if they responded to the good news of Jesus as Saul did? May that vision of a desired future version of them be an anchor for you as you consider how you might be a minister of reconciliation in their life.

CONNECT WITH JESUS THROUGH PRAYER

There is a famous scene in the Gospel of Mark where a man with an afflicted son approaches Jesus' disciples. The boy was held captive by a deeply embedded demonic power. The disciples try to help, but they fail. Exasperated, they go to Jesus, who shows his power by expelling the demon.

Afterward, the disciples ask Jesus why they weren't successful. They had done so before; why not this time? Jesus responds to their question by stating that this particular demonic force can only be cast out through prayer (Mark 9:29).

In this mission work we will be exposed to evil ideas and corrupt attitudes deeply embedded in people's hearts. If we are to engage our mission field in love and hope, we must anchor our hearts in Jesus through prayer.

Paul, writing to the Colossian church, asks them to "devote yourselves to prayer, being watchful and thankful. And pray for us, too, that God may open a door for our message so that we may proclaim the mystery of Christ, for which I am in chains. Pray that I may proclaim it clearly, as I should" (Colossians 4:2-4).

Connecting to Jesus in prayer is a humble act of submission to him, and an act of trust that he will empower us as we share the good news of the gospel with our mission field. Only by the power of Jesus can we pursue the work of reconciliation in peace and strength. In these times of prayer we can open our hearts, listening to his voice and remembering that he promises never to leave or forsake us. As you prepare to engage our mission field, I invite you to prioritize prayer.

A PRAYER FOR UPCOMING MEETINGS

This brief prayer is one I have used. It's based on Galatians 5:22-23 and 1 Corinthians 13:4-7. I encourage you to make it your own, incorporating your desires and perhaps Scripture that is meaningful to you. Regardless of the shape of your prayer, I hope that it will serve as an anchor for your soul as you set out to engage in the challenging work ahead.

Jesus, I am going to meet with [the person's name], who I know you love.

I pray that by the power of your Spirit, I might practice love, joy, peace, patience, kindness, goodness, faithfulness, gentleness, and self-control today.

Please grant me the strength to be patient and kind, not arrogant or proud.

Protect me from being easily angered and keeping a record of wrongs.

I pray that my words and attitude will not dishonor them.

I also know that you love me. That you delight in me. That you promise to be with me always.

I know that you are with me now.

May your love for me, my love for you, and our love for [person's name] allow me to delight in the truth, rest in hope, and persevere in faith.

Amen.

CHECK IN WITH YOUR HEART

As you spend time with the Lord, I encourage you to invite him to check in with your heart. Ask him to reveal what's going on within your soul. Proverbs 4:23 says, "Above all else, guard your heart, for everything you do flows from it." Our attitudes, actions, and convictions all flow from the heart. If it is not in the right place when we engage our mission field, we will likely do more harm than good.

My friend Ted is the founder of the Spiritual Formation Society of Arizona. He has provided me (and many others) with insightful questions for prayer and reflection. Here I offer a slightly modified version of Ted's heart-check questions. I invite you to prayerfully consider these questions and their related Scriptures before engaging with your mission field.

► Is my heart divided? (James 1)

► Am I brokenhearted? Holding onto pain, resentment, or hurt? (Psalm 147:3)

► Am I noticing any bitterness toward those I intend to reach? (Hebrews 12:14)

► Am I feeling anxious about meeting with this person? (Matthew 6:25-34)

▶ Have I hardened my heart to any person, circumstance, or emotion? (Mark 4)

After considering these things, listen to the Holy Spirit. Is there something else that God wants you to see?

I hope that these questions will help you identify what you are feeling and understand what is going on in your soul. I know that for some of us, talking about feelings can be a turnoff, but feelings are gifts from God. They are designed to help us know ourselves more truly. Counselor and author Chip Dodd says that feelings are the *voices of our hearts.* They are not impulses to control but rather the way God has designed us to connect with our deeper self, to understand our needs, desires, and hopes.

Dodd argues that there are eight core feelings: hurt, loneliness, sadness, anger, fear, shame, guilt, and gladness. He notes, "These eight core feelings are the beginning of the expression of all human emotional experience."[1] The ability to identify our feelings will help us gauge the health of our souls as we do the work of a missionary.

As you consider engaging your mission field, notice what you are feeling. There is nothing to fix or solve. Just notice. If the feeling is unusually powerful, consider taking that to the Lord in prayer. In praying through your feelings, ask the Lord to help you see what it is pointing to. There may be a deep need, hope, or desire that feels threatened when you consider meeting with the person in our mission field.

It is also important to recognize that the people of our mission field are also experiencing powerful emotions. American Christian nationalist leaders are skilled at cultivating feelings of anxiety, fear, shame, sadness, grief, and rage within their audiences to manipulate them. We can show love and hospitality by being attentive both to what we are feeling and what we perceive them to be feeling. When we approach our mission field, we want to do so from a place of health and rest in the Lord, a place of peace and confidence in Jesus.

One of the more difficult realities of our mission field is that the people are often close to us. They are coworkers, neighbors, close friends, and sometimes family. They are not strangers. We often know each other well. Because of this deep knowing, we may experience resentment that they have embraced American Christian nationalism. We may feel embarrassed or ashamed of them because their decisions may implicate us. Early on in my encounters with American Christian nationalism, I frequently felt disgust and outrage at the fact that this movement tore into pieces my friendships, community, and church.

I hated it for what it was doing to the people I loved. I hated the fact that I was disassociating from people that I had known for decades.

My initial attitude was militant, seeking to destroy the idea and those who believed it. I hated American Christian nationalism, and frankly, I hated those who gave themselves over to it.

This posture stole my joy, increased anxiety, multiplied despair, and ultimately took my eyes off Jesus. I also discovered that this resentment, embarrassment, shame, and rage were ultimately a *me* problem, not a *them* problem. Most of the work that needed to be done was in me, not them. I needed to work on my heart with Jesus and return to a place of peace, rest, and confidence in the Lord.

Because our mission field is so close to home, we must be vigilant and cautious in checking in with our hearts, ensuring that we are not motivated by resentment, outrage, or shame but rather by a genuine desire and love for those we seek to reach.

We are not saviors. We are not the ones who got it right. As has often been said, we are just one beggar telling another beggar where to find bread.

GET SOME REST

Engaging with our mission field can be emotionally and spiritually draining. God designed us for work and rest. In the earliest portions of Scripture we discover that cycles of work and rest (e.g., the sabbath, seasons, feast days) are woven into the fabric of creation and are good for our bodies, minds, and souls.

When adding a missional gathering to the calendar, consider adding time to rest before the event. A good night's sleep, a nap, or just some downtime are investments in your health and the mission field we seek to reach. A worn-out missionary will likely do more harm than good and may even give way to rage, anxiety, or fear.

RECRUIT A SUPPORT TEAM

I have been blessed to receive coaching from a lot of great crosscultural missionaries. One man in particular stands out to me. He has been serving in various mission fields for more than sixty years. He helped start new churches, guided them as they connected with local communities, and trained and supported younger missionaries.

During one of our conversations, he reminded me that mission work often puts a great deal of stress on a person's body, mind, and soul. To guard against burnout and despair, he strongly encouraged me to form a support team of friends, mentors, and ministry partners who would commit to praying for me, encouraging me, and reminding me of God's love for me and for those I was working to reach. This advice has proven to be invaluable.

One of the most powerful tools we have in this work is each other. We were made to be in communion with God and others. Support teams can take on many different forms. This includes but is not limited to the following:

- ▶ *Standing meetings.* This could be a weekly coffee with a group of close friends, a monthly breakfast with a mentor, or a periodic video call with teammates who share a similar burden to reach American Chrisitan nationalists. Scheduling time for a standing meeting can build a rhythm of encouragement, support, and prayer.

- ▶ *Prayer partners.* Recruit a handful of partners who will commit to pray with you for your ministry and for specific people you are working to reach. Before entering a difficult conversation, invite your prayer team to pray for those you will meet, and then follow up with a recap of the discussion and an invitation to keep praying for those you connected with.

► *Email newsletter.* Send a monthly email update to a consistent group, asking for specific prayer needs, and sharing updates on past prayer requests. These emails can guide your prayer partners and supporters in how to best pray for and encourage you.

SAFETY AND SELF-CARE

Hurt versus harm. Encounters with American Christian nationalists can be uncomfortable, tense, frustrating, and perhaps even threatening. We may experience pain from attacks or abuse. While some of these feelings may be hurtful, others can cause real harm. It is important to distinguish between the two for our health and longevity.

Hurt is a physical or emotional feeling of discomfort; *harm* is injury or damage. Although the distinction between the two can be difficult to discern, I suspect you may be able to intuitively understand the difference.[2]

Imagine that one day you decide to go to the gym to do some work on the bench press. As you approach the equipment, you load up some weights, lay on the padded bench, and put your hands on the gritty bar. You lift it off the stand and begin to feel the pain of carrying the weight. As you bring the bar down to your chest and begin to push the bar back up into the air, you feel something in your chest and arms. Pain!

This hurts, but it is a good hurt. It is the natural feeling of discomfort that happens when our muscles tear down to be rebuilt. This is a healthy process of muscle growth. Though you feel discomfort, pressing on and growing through the pain is healthy.

However, imagine that you had poor form when lifting. Perhaps you failed to appropriately stretch or put too much weight on the bar. As you lift, you feel a sharp pain shoot through your body. Everything in you says, *Stop!* You are experiencing harm, an unhealthy pain that will lead to further damage if you continue exercising. When you feel harm, it is time to put down the weights and take time to heal. The harm may be so severe that you need to seek professional help.

When doing physical exercise, it is important to listen to your body and discern if the pain you experience is hurt or harm. When engaging in mission work, knowing the difference between hurt and harm in our souls is crucial to continue the work in a way that is healthy for us and for those we seek to reach.

This is especially important for those who may be targeted by American Christian nationalist rhetoric, such as people of color, immigrants, refugees, Muslims, Democrats, and so on. As a straight, White, evangelical male I recognize that it is not usually a big risk for me to be in American Christian nationalist spaces. When I engage with this mission field, I rarely feel personally threatened (though it has happened on occasion).

Many of us desire to engage American Christian nationalists but are not able to do so without experiencing harm. Pamela Cooper-White notes that before we even begin a conversation, we must "determine whether fruitful conversation is possible. The first point of discernment is: Am I the right person to have this conversation with this person?"[3] If engaging people who adhere to American Christian nationalism is not safe, it may be both wise and loving to abstain from this work and trust that Jesus will bring someone into their life who is in a position to minister to them in safe, healthy ways. Like cross-cultural mission work, some of us are called to engage directly with a mission field while others are called to a support role, providing encouragement, prayer, and resources. Both of these roles, those who are sent and those who provide support, are crucial to the work. The sent ones cannot do their work apart from the prayer, encouragement, and energy of the supporters. As we see in Scripture, we are all one body with many parts, each playing a vital role in the work that God has for his church (Ephesians 4).

Walking away. While heart-to-heart conversations can be enriching and fruitful, they can also quickly fall apart. There may be occasions when you are conversing with someone, and they continually revert to combative rhetoric, anxious rants, or expressions of outrage. This is common in our mission field. Many American Christian nationalist leaders disciple their followers to behave in this way. However, if you are finding that there is no progress being made, it is likely time to consider whether this conversation is fruitful or not. Perhaps your conversation partner is not in a space to engage in heart-to-heart communication or is simply unwilling to engage in good-faith discussion.

When you arrive at these moments, I invite you to ask God to help you discern whether you should keep the conversation going or walk away. Unfortunately, I don't know of a playbook we can use to determine whether we should stay in a conversation or leave. It requires Jesus-centered wisdom and a heart guided by the Spirit of God.

If you find yourself in a space where you feel exasperated or exhausted, it may be wise to ask permission to pause the conversation so that you can have time to pray and consider the things discussed. If you believe it is safe to do so, I encourage you to strive for hospitality, letting them know that you desire to continue in good-faith conversations with them in the future if you can do so without harmful rhetoric or combative attitudes.

If not, that is okay.

Walking away doesn't mean you are giving up on the person. It simply means you are not the right conversation partner at this moment. You have not failed. God has not failed. There is still hope. If you are not in a position to continue the conversation with someone, I invite you to instead invest your energy in praying for them even more, and perhaps asking God to bring someone into their life that would continue the conversation and lead them back to the way of Jesus.

The apostle Paul encourages us to recognize that we are all part of a bigger plan of restoration. It may be that our role was to simply plant the seeds of repentance that someone else would water, and another would harvest. Writing to the church in Corinth, Paul says that we are to focus on the role

the Lord has assigned to each. I planted the seed, Apollos [another church leader] watered it, but God has been making it grow. So neither the one who plants nor the one who waters is anything, but only God, who makes things grow. The one who plants and the one who waters have one purpose, and they will each be rewarded according to their own labor. For we are co-workers in God's service. (1 Corinthians 3:5-9)

We are coworkers in God's ultimate plan. It may be that you have planted a seed that someone else will cultivate. The value of our work is seen in our faithfulness in the moment, not in the fruit that we get to see harvested. Though you may not see the fruit, your faithful labor is not in vain. As my friend Warren says, "God is faithful."

WHAT ABOUT THE CHILDREN?

As a father of four amazing kids I am concerned about the things they are exposed to, whether it's through Netflix, YouTube, peers at school, or the people we invite into our home. If you are a fellow parent, you know some of these decisions are relatively easy ("no, you cannot watch *Nightmare on Elm Street*"). Others are more difficult, especially regarding those we share our lives with. Following the way of Jesus, leading with hospitality, and inviting people into our homes can sometimes present a dilemma: I want to show hospitality to this person and welcome them into my home, but frankly I don't want my kids hearing the things they say.

I remember one event I hosted that included a variety of guests, some who promote American Christian nationalism. About an hour into the gathering, some of them began to bemoan regulations related to the Covid-19 pandemic. They boasted about the ways they refused to participate in them, even when in the presence of medically vulnerable people. They used slanderous language to talk about people who disagreed with them and made dehumanizing statements about people who wore masks. While I understand perspectives on masking vary from person to person, the arrogant, gloating, and belittling language got to me. I remember thinking, *I don't want my kids hearing this.*

Since then I've been careful to set healthy boundaries around who gets to be in the room and the type of language that is permitted around my family. This was my circumstance. You will likely face your own. It is both wise and loving for you and those you hope to reach to set healthy boundaries. In a situation such as this I could set boundaries on the conversation: "We don't use dehumanizing language in this house." Another option is to relegate my involvement with this group to spaces where my children will not be present. There are likely many other great options that you will discover.

If you are raising children, consider proper boundaries and methods that will align with your values while raising them. Like the children of crosscultural missionaries, they likely will be exposed to many ideas, postures, and perspectives that do not align with your family's values. Depending on the child(ren)'s maturity, consider your role in creating healthy boundaries to protect them. As they mature, think about ways you can involve them in the mission work you are doing while, at the same time, giving a lot of time and space for preparation and debriefing conversations with them. This is especially important when working to reach family members and close friends that your children know.

7

ENGAGING LEVIATHAN

A Field Guide

> [Christian nationalism is] an ideology that idealizes and
> advocates a fusion of American civic life with a particular type
> of Christian identity and culture. . . . The explicit ideological
> content of Christian nationalism comprises beliefs about historical
> identity, cultural preeminence, and political influence.
>
> ANDREW L. WHITEHEAD AND SAMUEL L. PERRY,
> *TAKING AMERICA BACK FOR GOD*

IN THIS CHAPTER WE WILL EXPLORE some of the most popular statements used by American Christian nationalists accompanied by suggestions for responding in a way that exposes how they are inconsistent with the teaching of Scripture and that leads to deeper, heart-to-heart conversations.

You may experience these statements in different forms, and I encourage you to adjust your responses accordingly. If possible, strive to have these conversations in person. Social media, email, and telephone rob us of the vital communication tools of facial expressions and body language. These suggested responses are not designed to help you win an argument but to build a bridge toward heart-to-heart conversations.

Before we get to the meat of the field guide, I invite you to join me in a brief retelling of one of my experiences at a Christian nationalist conference to gain a better understanding of what our mission field is hearing from their political leaders, media figures and, sadly, even their pastors.

SWIMMING WITH LEVIATHAN: MY TIME AT THE CHRISTIAN NATIONALIST PASTOR SUMMIT

It was an uncomfortably hot mid-August day when I packed the car and drove across the Sonoran Desert to San Diego to participate in the first-ever pastors' summit hosted by Turning Point USA. My goal was to connect with my fellow clergy and discover their motivation for joining the event, their relationship with TPUSA, and how they reconcile American Christian nationalism with the teachings of Scripture and their pastoral vocation. After checking in at the beautiful Loews Coronado Bay Resort, I found my way to the registration table where a dozen banners announcing the TPUSA Faith Pastors Conference assured me I was in the right place.

A cheerful group of young people greeted me and facilitated the check-in process. (In my experience most of the TPUSA staff are highly energetic, earnest, and kind college-aged men and women.) After obtaining my name tag and swag bag, I transitioned to the main ballroom where self-proclaimed Christian nationalist musician Sean Feucht was opening the summit in worship. It was announced that this gathering of over five hundred pastors was here to worship, stand for truth, and turn our country back to God.

The big idea. The throughline of the event was rallying the church to take government power and secure a future for our families and our faith. They argued that God established three institutions: the government, the church, and the family, and that for the last fifty years pastors were focused so much on the family and the church they abandoned the government to the progressive left, who are working to use government to corrupt the family and eradicate the church.

Therefore, they argued that pastors must encourage their people to fight the liberal regime and take back government power to protect the church and family.[1] During the three-day event, over twenty-five speakers presented in rapid-fire succession (no breaks other than lunch) and were loosely organized by topic.

Abortion. Multiple pro-life speakers presented abortion as genocide, often using inflammatory language (e.g., slaughter, butcher, torn limb-from-limb). Anti-abortion activist Lila Rose said, "'Love thy neighbor as thyself'—if you love your neighbor, you don't watch them be dismembered, dragged away to death, slaughtered. The slaughter is all around us."[2]

Pastors were encouraged to publicly condemn abortion as murder and to refer to those who advocate for abortion rights as murderous monsters.

School choice and Turning Point Christian Academy. Most speakers mentioned something about the evils of public school, often derisively referring to it as "government education." Many argued that the "woke Marxists" took over the school boards and teachers' unions and are now teaching children to hate God, their country, and themselves. Some explicitly called pastors to rally their people and take over the local school boards.[3]

David Barton, a fast-talking, humorous, self-educated and self-proclaimed historian, attributed America's moral decay to the failure of pastors to influence public schooling, saying, "The cesspool of America is coming out of the schools. The Church has been focused so much on family they forgot about the country . . . so the Left took control while we slept."[4]

Pastor Rick Brown of Kingdom X Consulting argued that the fight for public schools is a fight against evil: "While we are on earth, we will join together and destroy the devil. We will fight for the schools, the county supervisors."[5]

Sean Ellingson (husband of Lynsi Ellingson, owner of In-N-Out Burger) even cast doubt on private Christian schools, stating, "These Christian schools are cowardly. . . . [They are] not standing for truth."[6]

Hutz Hertzberg, chief education officer of Turning Point Christian Academy and the previous principal of the Christian Heritage Academy in Illinois, noted that public schools are "promoting the sexualization of our kids and grooming them. They promote CRT and vaccine mandates. These kids are sexually groomed and emotionally abused."

Hertzberg then argued that the best solution is for pastors to partner with TPUSA to launch a Turning Point Christian Academy on their church campus, not officially as a school but as an education ministry. Hertzberg argued, "This hybrid model takes the 'best of private education and the best of homeschooling.'" He also stated that because it is a ministry, not a school, it would avoid "a lot of government regulation."[7]

Religious liberty and Covid-19. Almost every speaker referred to "government overreach" into the church, citing as evidence Covid-19 restrictions such as prohibiting large gatherings, use of face masks, and social distancing. There were a lot of self-congratulatory stories highlighting various pastors refusing to shut down or "bow down to the government." Refusing to adhere to public health guidelines was portrayed as allegiance to God over the government because God wants the church to gather.

The kingdom of God and the church were often used synonymously and were envisioned as a large, gathered assembly in a big building on a Sunday morning. To my recollection there was no mention of the church as the people who follow Jesus or anything like Acts 2 style house churches. One of the clearest examples of this phenomenon came from Pastor Raul Ries who, while giving an impassioned gospel presentation, through tears said, "We [would not] close the doors of the church in 2020. . . . I will not close the doors to the kingdom of God."[8]

Taking government power. A key argument of the event was that Christians need to take back government power to protect the church and family. They stated that when the government is in the hands of non-Christians, it works to destroy the church and the family. This idea was reinforced in a few ways. First, they argued that America is a Christian nation. No nation on the earth has blessed the world as much as the United States. God has used America because we are a Christian country.

Pastor Rob McCoy went so far as to argue that "the [Greek] word that is translated as church is *ecclesia*. . . . Tyndale rightly translates *ecclesia* as 'assembly.' . . . Aristotle said *ecclesia* means the public square. The *ecclesia* is the public square, and the church abandoned it." McCoy seemed to argue that the New Testament authors understood the church to be synonymous with the public square, which, he implies, is the government.

McCoy summed up his perspective, stating, "The Lord is a nationalist. Look at the tower of Babel."[9]

Defiance. Audience members were often lauded for their courage in disobeying government restrictions related to Covid, advocating for specific conservative candidates from the pulpit (contrary to the Johnson Amendment, which prohibits 501(c)(3) non-profit organizations from endorsing or supporting political candidates), and for standing their ground on abortion and school choice in the face of cancel culture.

David Barton stated in a defiant tone, "The Johnson Amendment is technically not legal. We have been working with ADF (Alliance Defending Freedom) to try to get pastors sued to test it."[10]

The theme of defiance was reinforced by the frequent use of *us-them* rhetoric that seasoned many of the speeches. In speaking of the bright side of the Covid pandemic, Victor Marx, CEO of All Things Possible Ministries, stated, "Look at us. We found out who's who in the zoo."

He followed this statement with stories of pastors who had failed to stand up to the government. He shared that these were leaders he once respected, but now he openly resists: "I publicly called out pastors on social media. I have questioned a few guys I once respected . . . I've taken their books off my bookshelf."[11]

Militant rhetoric. To complement the theme of defiance, militant language was often invoked, much to the praise of this congregation of clergy.

- ▸ "God raises up leaders to defend the body of Christ." Rob McCoy[12]

- ▸ "Prepare yourself for the coming attack. We are more than conquerors." Rob McCoy[13]

- ▸ "The US Navy is the standard of righteousness in the world." Bob McEwan[14]

In a panel discussion, Pastor Rick Brown stated, "God is a god of war. The devil got into the schools, the FBI, the CDC . . . the wicked *stole* the gold from the Golden State."[15]

When asked what encouragement he would give to the room full of embattled pastors, Michael O'Fallon, founder of Sovereign Nations, rebuked the crowd: "We need men with chests. . . . You are standing by while the bride of Christ is being raped. It is time to stand."[16]

Church growth. Most of the pastors who gave presentations shared their recent successes in light of their stances in 2020.[17] Most intimated that in 2020 a large number of people left their congregation because of their political stance. However, because they took a stand for truth, their church attendance and budget have since grown exponentially.

In a session called "Jesus First," Luke Barnett, lead pastor of Dream City Church in Arizona, told a story that took place during the early days of the Covid-19 pandemic, when Charlie Kirk asked if he could host a Turning Point rally at Dream City Church. He happily agreed. To his surprise he discovered that President Donald Trump would be in attendance. Barnett shared the news with his staff and then told us that his entire worship team gave him an ultimatum: cancel the event, or they would resign.

At this point, a few dozen pastors in the room shouted in an antagonistic tone, "Byeeee!"

Barnett told us that he could not, in good conscience, cancel the event.

He then shared that 30 percent of Dream City Church's staff left along with 40 percent of the congregation due to his decision, but he then gladly shared that this decision brought about the "biggest season of growth ever. . . . We are winning conservative people to Christ. . . . We are winning big businesspeople. . . . We'd not be in the position we are in today [if not for our partnership with TPUSA]."[18]

Gary Hamrick, senior pastor of Cornerstone Chapel in Virginia stated, "When you stand for truth you either get revival or riot. We've had more baptisms, double the budget in the last two years. [It is a] revival!"[19]

Jurgen Matthesius, the lead pastor of Awaken Church in Southern California, shared a similar sentiment: "We kept meeting in 2020 and suicides went down, people got saved, [saying,] 'Thank God your church doors were open!' . . . We didn't mask, we didn't distance because we are a people that says, 'God has said' and we are *not* the people that say, 'Has God said?'"

He wrapped up this segment with the unfiltered proclamation: "We [Awaken Church] take a *pro-Trump* stance."[20]

Revisionist history. The influence of the Christian clergy on America's founding, growth, and power was invoked as a model for modern-day pastors. Bob McEwan claimed that the founders intended for Christians to influence the legislative body, citing Benjamin Franklin's call for there to be prayers in the assembly.[21]

David Barton proposed that America has been uniquely blessed by God because of the influence of Christianity. He argued, "No other nation in history has blessed the world like America has."

The proof? "Ninety-six percent of the world's inventions are from America," he said, followed by, "I believe in American exceptionalism. . . . We are different, we are the exception, not the rule." He went on to argue that America was made great because it was influenced by pastors. He claimed, "It was the pulpit that shaped the Declaration of Independence."[22]

Conclusion. While many of the quotes in this chapter are disturbing, they are also instructive. These leaders are masters at weaving Scripture together with their nationalistic views in a way that many of their hearers believe to be in accordance with Scripture. Before responding to the rhetoric, take a moment to consider that many in our mission field are hearing this rhetoric *all of the time.* Statements like these are parroted by various organizations, conferences, news outlets, social media channels, radio programs, and even Bible studies across the country.

Responding to these statements will require prayer, compassion, patience, and humble subversion.

A FIELD GUIDE FOR RESPONDING TO AMERICAN CHRISTIAN NATIONALISTS

In the remainder of this chapter we will explore some of the regularly used phrases of American Christian nationalists. Each section contains a statement with a bit of coaching, accompanied by clarifying questions, shared values, shibboleths, red flags, good things to honor, humble subversion, and occasionally resources and notes. These are not formulaic scripts but rather starting points for heart-to-heart conversations with your mission field, and I encourage you to customize them according to your context.

FIELD GUIDE LEGEND

The statement. I include popular versions of statements often repeated by American Christian nationalists.

Clarifying questions. Clarifying questions are neutral questions designed to deepen your knowledge of their understanding of the statement. This is one place we can work to truly grasp what they mean and how they see things.

Shared values. Once we understand where a Christian nationalist is coming from, we can look for ways to connect with them based on our shared values. I include some possible shared values, but the list is not exhaustive, and I invite you to discern your own.

Shibboleths and red flags. Included are words or phrases that could communicate "I am a friend" (shibboleths) or "I am an enemy" (red flags). Use accordingly. I don't include some of the more obvious red flags like "You are out of your mind" or "That is the dumbest thing I've ever heard." I assume you know these are not healthy or strategic.

Good things to honor. There are usually honorable values underneath the rhetoric of Christian nationalists. I provide some possible things to honor that are tethered to the specific statement.

Humble subversion. I include questions and responses designed to be invitations for our counterparts to engage in deeper thinking and perhaps even meditate on Scripture or the example of Jesus and how they apply to the related topic.

BEFORE WE BEGIN

These are not scientific categories. I have worked to organize the statements into a handful of categories. These exist to break the statements into manageable sections. They are not intended to be scientific categorizations, and some statements could easily fit in multiple categories. Don't worry too much about which section they fall under. Real-life conversations are not so neatly ordered.

The statements change over time. Keep in mind that American Christian nationalist rhetoric shifts over time. Some of the following statements will evolve or become outdated. As new statements appear I encourage you to learn from the following approach and apply the methods to what you are hearing in your conversations with our mission field.

These are not debate tactics. The suggested responses that follow are not designed to be used in debate. They are meant to cultivate deeper conversation, not win arguments. In a debate there is a winning team and a losing team. A missionary wants to guide conversations to Jesus so that everyone wins.

BIBLE VERSES

Advocates of American Christian nationalism frequently use Scripture to reinforce their propaganda. Though the quotes are taken from the Bible, they are used in ways that do not align with the author's original intent and sometimes directly contradict their initial purpose (see "Distorting God's Word" in chapter 3). Many in our mission field have a good desire to be shaped by Scripture but are likely unaware of the fuller context of these verses and the ways they have been misapplied. We can affirm this desire and encourage a deeper engagement with the text.

These texts and others like them deserve to be explored within their context before considering how we should live them out today. Christians throughout history have wrestled with how to best apply Scripture to daily life and public policy. It is not easy and requires patience, wisdom, and the guidance of the Holy Spirit. Scripture should shape our thinking on the important questions of our time. However, simply quoting a text and dogmatically applying it to my preferred policy position does injustice to the text and the broader community.

Second Chronicles 7:14. American Christian nationalists often connect the United States to Scriptures relating specifically to ancient Israel. Here's an example of an Old Testament verse they use incorrectly: "If my people, which are called by my name, shall humble themselves, and pray, and seek my face, and turn from their wicked ways; then will I hear from heaven, and will forgive their sin, and will heal their land" (2 Chronicles 7:14 KJV). They argue that like Israel, God has uniquely blessed and called America to a special purpose in human history, but our godless enemies (the libs) have taken power and are exerting their evil influence over us, pushing our country away from God. They believe this puts God's calling on our people in jeopardy and places our unique blessing at risk. They argue that we, the people of America, need to collectively turn back to God so he will continue to bless us. If we don't, God might destroy us or allow our enemies to be victorious.

Coaching notes. Conversations about Old Testament texts offer us two strategic opportunities. First, we can explore how Scripture can shape us today. Reading excerpts like 2 Chronicles 7:14 in the broader context of the Bible can lead to fruitful conversations about how God's relationship with ancient Israel can guide us today. While I do not believe that it is wise to uncritically apply God's promises to Israel to America, we can learn from their example and through prayer and careful Bible study apply certain principles to our modern lives.

I recommend inviting your conversation partners to join you in engaging with material from accessible Bible study resources like the Bible

Project, the BEMA podcast, and the Center for Hebraic Thought. For more information, visit https://disarmingleviathan.com.

Second, we can explore the breadth of God's instruction in the Old Testament, including the frequent calls for Israel to collectively confess their sin, a practice that happens in many churches around the world today (often called corporate confession).[23] When done well, this practice cultivates healthy solidarity with the marginalized and care for those who have suffered injustice and harm. While promoters of American Christian nationalism would balk at calls to corporate confession of institutionalized racism, chattel slavery, or Manifest Destiny, they frequently call for corporate confession for sexual licentiousness, abortion, and godlessness in general. We can help our conversation partners broaden the scope of the sins that we publicly confess and think holistically about what it means to be a people who value repentance.[24]

Clarifying questions

- ► I love that you care about this so deeply. Tell me more about why this matters to you.

- ► Who do you think the "my people" in the verse is referring to?

- ► What do you think it would look like if America were to "seek God's face and turn from their wicked ways"?

- ► How many people in America do you think would need to repent for God to heal our land?

Possible shared values

- ► A nation that honors God would indeed be a wonderful place to live.

- ► Public confession of sins, especially ones that have been historically done by Americans, is good.

Shibboleths

- ► I believe that confession of sin is healthy.

- ► I too pray that God heals the brokenness in our country.

- ► I want all of my fellow Americans to seek God.

Red flags

- ► The Old Testament is outdated and should not shape our modern life in America.

- ► You don't know how to read the Bible.

Good things to honor

- ► Applying the Scripture to modern-day issues is sometimes difficult, but very good!

- ► Wanting to honor God is good!

Humble subversion

- ► I love that you care deeply about learning from Scripture and applying it to our lives today. I think it'd be good to read this verse in context (read 2 Chronicles 6–8 together). Notice that God specifically addresses Solomon, the king of Israel. Is there anything in the text that implies this promise is intended for countries other than ancient Israel? What parts might be just for Israel? What principles can we apply in the church today?

- ► Do you think that American Christians are commanded to follow to the religious customs and methods of worship that God called ancient Israel to practice?

- ► Notice that God specifically calls Israel to live according to his statutes (which they often fail to do). What are those statutes?[25] Do they apply to us in the same way they applied to ancient Israel?

- ► If America is specifically chosen by God to obey his statutes, which ones do you think we should prioritize? God frequently commands his people to care for those on the margins like immigrants, widows, orphans, and the poor. How do you think those statutes should impact our policies and laws today?

- ► This text is a call to corporate repentance. If Americans humbled themselves and repented, what are the things that you think we, as a country, would need to repent of?

Luke 22:36. Many American Christian nationalists invoke Luke 22:36, "He that hath no sword, let him sell his garment, and buy one" (KJV) to advocate for stronger Second Amendment protections. This Scripture is often cited to promote the use of firearms, often in the context of defending one's family from criminals or government-sponsored tyranny. I have personally encountered this verse in speeches by gun-rights advocates, in propaganda at gun shows, and in a multitude of bumper stickers that often place the text atop silhouettes of assault rifles.

Coaching notes. At first glance the statement seems to show Jesus encouraging his disciples to obtain weapons for protection. However, when read in context we see that Jesus shows little faith in tools of violence to advance his purposes. If you read a little further, you will find that Jesus' statement that two swords are enough for the whole group undermines the power of weapons in the kingdom of God. While there are many different opinions of how Scripture shapes our views on instruments of violence, this text is not a clear endorsement of the use of firearms to protect ourselves or our communities.

Clarifying questions

- ▶ Tell me why this is important to you.
- ▶ What does it mean to "buy a sword" today?
- ▶ Why do you think Jesus said this to his disciples?
- ▶ Are there other portions of Scripture that show Jesus talking about the use of weapons?

Possible shared values

- ▶ Safety for the people I love.
- ▶ Loving others by protecting them from harm.

Shibboleths

- ▶ I own guns (if you do).
- ▶ I am not against gun ownership (if you are not).
- ▶ I'm not a pacifist (if you are not).

▶ The ability to protect yourself and others from people seeking to do violence is a good desire.

Red flags

▶ I hate guns. Guns are evil.

▶ The government should make firearms illegal to own.

▶ I don't think anyone should own a gun.

▶ People with guns are mentally unstable, bloodthirsty nutjobs.

Good things to honor

▶ Safety from harm is a core human need.

▶ The desire to stop people from committing acts of violence is good.

▶ Gun enthusiasts will share that many firearms are used for sport or hunting and are connected to caring for one's family.[26] Depending on your perspective, this could be a good thing to honor.

Humble subversion. Before I get to the humbly subversive questions, I want to give some context to show how this could be studied with your conversation partner. The Scripture in question comes from the Gospel of Luke where we find Jesus about to be arrested. He reminds his disciples that he has always provided for them, and now he is giving them instructions on how to prepare for the days ahead:

> He said to them, "But now if you have a purse, take it, and also a bag; and if you don't have a sword, sell your cloak and buy one. It is written: 'And he was numbered with the transgressors'; and I tell you that this must be fulfilled in me. Yes, what is written about me is reaching its fulfillment."
>
> The disciples said, "See, Lord, here are *two swords*."
>
> "*That's enough!*" he replied.
>
> Jesus went out as usual to the Mount of Olives, and his disciples followed him. (Luke 22:36-39, emphasis added)

Notice how many swords Jesus says is enough: *two.* Two swords for the whole group? Jesus is definitely not preparing his followers for an armed revolt. Look at what happens next.

> While he was still speaking, a crowd came up, and the man who
> was called Judas, one of the Twelve, was leading them. He ap-
> proached Jesus to kiss him, but Jesus asked him, "Judas, are you
> betraying the Son of Man with a kiss?"
>
> When Jesus' followers saw what was going to happen, they said,
> *"Lord, should we strike with our swords?"* And one of them struck
> the servant of the high priest, cutting off his right ear.
>
> But Jesus responded, *"No more of this!"* And he touched the
> man's ear and healed him. (Luke 22: 47-51, emphasis added)

Notice that Jesus does not call his followers to take up arms against
the mob that came to arrest him. Instead, he tells them to put their
swords away. Jesus even heals the victim of his disciple's violent
action. The Gospel of Matthew's account of this scene adds these
words from Jesus: "Put your sword back in its place . . . for all who
draw the sword will die by the sword" (Matthew 26:52). When read in
context, we discover that Jesus undermines the power of the sword.
Now to the questions.

- ▶ I am so glad that you care deeply about the safety of your family
  and our community. I too believe that protecting ourselves and
  others from violence is a good thing. I also know that Jesus warned
  his followers about the deceptive and destructive power of violence. Remember when he said, "All who draw the sword will die
  by the sword"? He also said things like "turn the other cheek" and
  even gave himself over to the people who wanted to kill him. I feel
  conflicted between my desire for safety and the call of Jesus to put
  down our swords. What do you think?

- ▶ While Jesus does tell his followers to buy a sword if they don't have
  one, he says that two is enough for the whole group. I wonder if
  this statement shows some form of moderation for the amount of
  sword power they should use. How do you think this might influence our thinking on firearm regulations?

- ▶ Many of the earliest followers of Jesus were martyred for their
  faith. Though they faced opposition from the Roman Empire,

many did not advocate taking up arms to protect themselves or their beliefs. How do you think their example should shape our thinking today?

John 15:13. "Greater love hath no man than this, that a man lay down his life for his friends" (John 15:13 KJV). This text is often invoked to honor police officers or those who serve in the armed services. One popular bumper sticker features silhouettes of a modern soldier and a Jesus-like figure on the cross and states, "There are only two men that have given their life for you: the American Soldier and Jesus Christ." An online retailer sells a picture of a police officer flanked by angels' wings and an American flag atop this text from John 15:13.[27] These images conflate the crucifixion of Jesus with the sacrifice of the men and women in uniform. This has the effect of sanctifying their vocation. In some cases this leads to a refusal to critique unjust actions perpetrated by those serving in these vocations.

Coaching notes. While there are varying perspectives on how and if followers of Jesus should engage in acts of violence, we can honor the sacrifice of those who serve in vocations that require them to risk their lives in the service of others. We do so, however, without treating them as inherently sacred.

In our conversations we want to show that the death of Jesus is unique. He is God in the flesh who died for the sins of the whole world (1 John 2:1-2). Equating a soldier or police officer's sacrifice with that of Jesus distorts the gospel.[28] On a personal note, as a pastor I have had the honor of ministering to dozens of military veterans and law enforcement officers in the congregation I serve. None of them have equated their service or the sacrifice of their comrades with the death of Jesus. Most of them have recoiled at the idea.

Many people in our mission field will dismiss criticism of the US military or the seventeen thousand law enforcement agencies as unpatriotic or even sacrilegious.[29] In our discussions we can invite our conversation partners to study the Scripture with us and perhaps discover a nuanced Jesus-centered wisdom that honors the good and condemns the bad.

Note. During the Vietnam era, many American soldiers were dishonored as they returned home, partly due to the lack of trust in the federal government's reasons for being in Vietnam and some war crimes that made headline news. Today, many who seek to honor veterans recognize this and strive to show honor in any way possible. This often means that critiques of America's military are viewed as an act of dishonor. I encourage you to prayerfully consider how you might in good faith honor the people (many are quite young) who serve or have served and also call out America's unjust use of military power in our history and present day.

Clarifying questions

- ► What is the original context of this verse?

- ► What do you think Jesus means when he says this?

Possible shared values

- ► Sacrificially serving one's country is good.

- ► We should honor those who have served in the military or police force.

Shibboleths

- ► I have a great deal of respect for those who serve in the armed services and law enforcement.

- ► I am so thankful for the people who have given their lives in service to our country.

- ► If possible, share a story about visiting a veterans' cemetery, serving at a veterans' hospital, or something similar.

Red flags

- ► Anyone who does violence as part of their job is evil.

- ► Soldiers (or police) are just bloodthirsty, violent killers.

- ► Cops (or soldiers) are power-hungry bullies.

- ► We should defund the police (or the Department of Defense).

Good things to honor

► Sacrificially giving one's life to protect others can be a loving action, especially in a broken world where there is so much evil and violence.

► Putting one's life on the line in the service of others is both honorable and good.

Humble subversion

► I am so glad that you care about the soldiers and police who serve our country. I greatly value the men and women who have given their lives in the service of others. I mourn the loss of their death, and I want to honor their sacrifice. [Perhaps tell a story of how you've done that or share a story of someone you know who has died in the line of duty.] However, as I read the words of Jesus in John 15, it seems like Jesus is talking specifically about his sacrificial death on the cross for the world's sins. I wonder if using that statement in the context of military service or law enforcement is appropriate. What do you think?

► While I honor those who serve in the line of duty, I know that there can sometimes be bad actors in the police force or American military, as there are in any line of work. In Luke 3:14 John the Baptist tells soldiers not to steal and to live justly. To me this implies that those in positions of power can be tempted to take advantage of people or even commit evil against those they are called to serve. How should this teaching influence our response when soldiers or law enforcement officers commit acts of injustice?

► I support the men and women in uniform. They put their lives on the line to protect our country. As a Christian I want everyone, all around the world, to meet Jesus and follow him. I have been reflecting on the choice to call America a Christian nation. Suppose our military engages in violence against a community in a foreign country, and the people in that country see American Christians uncritically celebrating their military. How might that affect the ability of our missionaries to share the good news of Jesus with them?

THEOLOGICAL STATEMENTS

While not quoting Scripture directly, these statements contain theological beliefs. As this is a field guide, we will not get too deep into the theological debates underneath each statement; instead, we will focus on how to engage our mission field in heart-to-heart communication. In our conversations we can honor the fact that those in our mission field want to apply their faith to their politics. We can use these opportunities to develop a deeper, more robust theological perspective on the issues we face in our lives.

America should be a Christian nation. While this principle can also be framed as "America is Christian" or "The founders intended America to be a Christian nation," it speaks to a core belief of American Christian nationalism, namely, that the United States should recognize Christianity as its official religion and should work to protect the church and promote Christian values. They often tether this with an argument that God has called America to be a beacon of godliness and that God will uniquely work through the United States to accomplish his purposes if we remain devoted to him.

Coaching notes. This claim is a central argument of American Christian nationalist advocates (see "What is American Christian nationalism?" in chapter 2). In conversations with our mission field we want to do three things. First, affirm the desire for people in our country to love, follow, and live like Jesus and for our culture and laws to be just and virtuous.

Second, we want to invite our hearers to consider the best way for Christians to influence the government and the broader culture. Throughout Scripture and church history this is accomplished through self-sacrificial love and service to others, especially those on the margins.

Last, we want to discern if establishing a Christian nation is something the Scriptures call for or is even possible. Just because many Christians serve in government does not make the government's actions inherently Christian.

In conversations about Christian involvement in politics, I encourage you to be clear that you are not advocating that we should abstain from serving in government (unless that is your conviction). Rather, we can encourage our hearers to consider how the Scriptures call followers of Jesus to take on the form of a servant, especially when they are in positions of power (see the "Political Creatures" in chapter 4).

Clarifying questions

▶ Tell me why this matters to you.

▶ What do you think it means for America to be a Christian nation?

▶ What are the identifying markers of a Christian nation?

▶ What parts of Scripture do you believe advocate for the idea of a Christian nation?

Possible shared values

▶ I think that it would be amazing if all Americans followed Jesus.

▶ I would love America's laws and culture to be shaped by the Christian values of love, grace, humility, justice, and truth.

Shibboleths

▶ I pray that God will continue to bless America.

▶ I want people in America to follow Jesus.

Red flags

▶ America is a secular state and needs to stay that way.

▶ Religion should have no influence on our politics.

Good things to honor

▶ A country in which most or all citizens live out the values of Jesus would be good for all its inhabitants.

► The desire to see people in our country follow Jesus is good.

► It is good for countries to organize their laws in ways that lead to human flourishing.

Humble subversion

► I am so grateful that you want our nation to love and follow Jesus. I too long for the day when all of our neighbors embody righteousness and justice. I've been wondering how our culture might be different if everyone embodied the fruit of the Spirit (Galatians 5:22-23). What do you think that would be like?

► Thinking about our government, I agree that it would be awesome to have wise, faithful followers of Jesus in charge. That would be a true blessing to so many people. I've been thinking about how they would live out their faith while serving in positions of power. How do you think Jesus' teachings like the Sermon on the Mount (Matthew 5–7) should shape the hearts and minds of Christians who lead our country?

► I've heard you use the term *Christian nation* and I was wondering if there is a section of Scripture you've found that encourages Christians to establish a government. If so, I'd love to study it with you.

► I have been thinking about American missionaries around the world. If the United States claims to be Christian and then does acts of violence (like waterboarding or killing civilians), I wonder how that might compromise the witness of our missionaries serving abroad. What do you think?

We need to worship God, not government. Some American Christian nationalists argue that secular liberal elites are attempting to force Americans to worship the federal government instead of God. They point to what they believe are secular policies that expand the reach and power of the federal government as evidence that those on the left want the government to become godlike. When our mission field hears Democrats extol the virtues of healthy government and the ability of people to foster change through government policies, they interpret it as a false gospel.

Coaching notes. Worshiping the power of one's people is a very real phenomenon (see "American Christian Nationalism Can Lead to Empire Worship" in chapter 4). However, it is not only a temptation for progressives. Americans on all sides of the political matrix can be tempted to worship the greatness of the United States. The key question for Christians is, Am I being tempted to place my trust in the power and might of the government over that of Jesus? The irony is that American Christian nationalism argues that Christians should take over the government so that it can use its power to protect Christian families and promote the faith. So even in spite of their long-standing distrust of its sovereignty, they ultimately place more trust in government than in Christ and his church to transform culture.

In our conversations we can affirm the truth that it is better to worship the one true God and not the government. We can reinforce the value of introspection, considering the ways that I might be tempted to trust too much in a political leader or party to bring about true Christlike change in our communities. We can ask if there are any leaders today who are demanding total allegiance to a cause or movement, pointing out that both the progressives and conservatives can be tempted to assume this posture. Finally, we can remind ourselves and our conversation partners of how good it is when we give our ultimate allegiance to Jesus, the King of the cosmos!

Clarifying questions

- ► Tell me why this is important to you.

- ► Who are the people you hear advocating for the worship of government over God?

- ► What does government worship look like in America?

Possible shared values

- ► Worshiping God is good.

- ► Government is not God.

Shibboleths

- ▸ It is certainly tempting to revere or place absolute trust in political power.

- ▸ My understanding is that the early church was often pressured to worship Caesar as a god. Worshiping the power of one's country was bad then, and it is bad now.

Red flags

- ▸ No one worships the government today.

- ▸ The government does not pose a threat to Christians today.

Good things to honor

- ▸ Worshiping God is good. Certainly, one's government is a poor substitute for the living God!

- ▸ Our ultimate allegiance is to Jesus, not the government.

Humble subversion

- ▸ I love that you take this so seriously. I do too, and I agree that worship of political power can be very tempting. Throughout human history people have been tempted to worship their empire. In the Bible we find kings like Nebuchadnezzar telling people to worship him (Daniel 3). I think I remember hearing somewhere that Caesar was often worshiped as a god. That is destructive to any society and especially hurts people on the margins. In what ways can we Americans (arguably one of the most economically and militarily powerful governments in the world today) guard ourselves from empire worship?

- ▸ What would be some ways that our leaders could help us focus less on the greatness of our country and more on the greatness of God?

- ▸ I've been thinking a lot about what the Scripture teaches about honoring our leaders. First Peter 2:17 says that followers of Jesus should "fear God [and] honor the emperor." I have heard that Roman emperors were often worshiped as gods. I've been wrestling with how I can both fear and worship God while also honoring government leaders, especially when they behave in ungodly ways. What do you think?

Christians need to take control. The call to forcefully obtain positions of authority within society has various forms that include taking control of the school board, the federal government, the media, and the culture (by way of winning the culture wars). While there are a multitude of movements seeking political dominance, American Christian nationalists bolster their power-seeking with a theological belief called Christian dominionism.[30]

Modern forms of dominionism (such as the Seven Mountain Mandate) argue that Christians should work to assume control of all key segments of society—entertainment, business, education, family, government, media, and religion—to establish a godly country.

This movement (begun in the 1970s by leaders like C. Peter Wagner) has grown in popularity over the last five decades, spread by modern-day religious influencers like Lance Wallnau and Andrew Wommack, and political leaders like Representative Lauren Boebert. American Christian nationalists frequently use the language and principles of the Seven Mountain Mandate, such as "fighting the culture war" and "taking America Back for God."[31]

Coaching notes. Earlier in the book, we saw that American Christian nationalist leaders promote sword power over cross power to influence society (see "American Christian Nationalism Relies on the Power of the Sword" in chapter 4). While the statement "take control" relies on a powering-over posture, some of the underlying concerns are good. Many people want to make sure their society is righteous, just, and honoring to God. These are good desires, and we can affirm them in our conversations while at the same time confronting the powering-over posture and showing them that the ways of Jesus are ultimately the only way to cultivate cultural renewal.

Clarifying questions

- ► What would "taking control" look like?
- ► What methods should we use to take dominion over these "mountains" of culture?

Possible shared values

- ▶ I believe it would be good if those in power in these various segments of culture were shaped by the way of Jesus.

- ▶ I agree that culture is often shaped by institutions in the various spheres of society, and it would be good for them to be in alignment with the teachings of Jesus.

Shibboleths

- ▶ I think it would be good for followers of Jesus to serve in all aspects of society.

- ▶ Jeremiah 29 says we should seek the peace and prosperity of the places we live in. I think it is good for Christians to work toward the peace and prosperity of our country in these various parts of society.

Red flags

- ▶ I don't think Christians should be in control of anything.

- ▶ These institutions don't matter; we should just focus on the hearts of people.

Good things to honor

- ▶ Followers of Jesus living the Jesus way can be a blessing to all these areas of society.

- ▶ Striving to honor God with every aspect of our lives is really good.

Humble subversion

- ▶ I love that you are thinking about how the way of Jesus can transform society. I share many of your concerns. Lately, I've been thinking about the teachings of Jesus. He seems to frequently call his followers to serve others, go the extra mile, pray for their enemies, and so on. How do you think his example could shape our ideas of cultural renewal?

- ▶ I hear people talking about how Christians should control the culture so they can make the United States a Christian nation. I long for the day when we live in a culture shaped by the gospel. However, I've been wondering what is the best method for cultivating Jesus-centered change in society. I've been reading the Bible lately and I can't find anything that argues for a top-down, take-over-the-institutions approach. Instead, it seems like the recurring theme of the Bible is for Christians to spread the hope of the gospel by living out the teachings of Jesus within the church and inviting others to join. The early Christians emphasized sacrificial service, generosity, and love toward their neighbors. They even sought ways to honor their pagan government rulers (e.g., Philippians 2; 2 Timothy 2; 2 Peter 2). How do you think their example should shape us today?

▶ I agree that many segments of our society promote beliefs and attitudes that are unjust and unrighteous. In a sense I feel like they are my enemies. My instinct is to defeat them, but I've been thinking about what Jesus said about loving my enemies (Matthew 5:43-44). I think Jesus wants us to sacrificially love and serve even the people we think are promoting evil. Would you read the Sermon on the Mount (Matthew 5–7) with me and let's talk about how it might influence our understanding of how to respond to the corrupt aspects of our culture today?

POLITICAL STATEMENTS

This section includes common statements that come up frequently in discussions about politics and government policies. While political in nature, they are more dismissive slanders than thoughtful policy arguments. In chapter two I argued that while Christian nationalism is a political ideology, most American Christian nationalist leaders are not promoting thoughtful government policies but are instead using political lingo to foster anxiety and rage.

Immigrants are ruining America. Statements like "immigrants are ruining America" are often targeted against non-White immigrants, asylum seekers, and refugees.[32] The underlying anxiety stems from a belief that *they* are bringing foreign cultures, languages, and practices into America and will eventually eradicate the American way of life. Many American Christian nationalist leaders capitalize on instances of violence and use them to paint immigrants as criminals. They warn their hearers that there is a flood of illegal immigrants invading our country seeking to rape and pillage our neighborhoods.

Coaching notes. This topic can be especially difficult to navigate because our conversation partners will often use racist and xenophobic rhetoric. Knowing how and when to call someone out on bigoted statements will require guidance from the Spirit (see chapter 6). One of the primary goals in the following conversations is to humanize immigrants and reconnect our hearers with their family's immigration story.

Clarifying questions

- ► Why is this important to you?

- ► Are there negative changes you have noticed in our community that were caused by immigrants?

- ► Are there specific immigrants you have in mind?

- ► In what ways are they negatively impacting our community?

Possible shared values

- ► Care for our neighbors.

- ► A desire to be safe from people who would do evil in our community.

Shibboleths

- ► I am also concerned about the well-being of our community.

- ► I believe our government should protect the lives and livelihood of its citizens.

Red flags

- ► Globalization is inevitable.

- ► We should have open borders.

- ► You are blowing this out of proportion.

Good things to honor

▶ The values of hard work, justice, mercy, community, and the like.

▶ Ensuring economic stability for our community.

▶ Providing safety for the community by working to keep bad actors out (e.g., border security, policing, etc.).

Humble subversion

▶ I too believe that our government should work to protect us from people wanting to do evil in our community. However, I also know that immigrants are often fleeing from harm, just as Jesus' family fled to Egypt to find safety from Herod's murderous threat (Matthew 2:13-23). America, like Egypt in Jesus' day, has a lot of financial resources and military might. I've been wrestling with our responsibility to use those resources to help protect people fleeing from bad situations. What do you think?

▶ When I hear statements about immigrants invading our country, I feel fear. But lately I've been thinking about the frequent commands in Scripture to care for foreigners in our community. Would you be willing to read some of these portions of Scripture with me and explore how they might shape our views of our posture toward immigrants?[33]

▶ I have been thinking about my ancestry. Do you know yours? Where do your people come from? Did they migrate to America? If so, where were they from? What was their immigrant journey like? What were the circumstances that caused them to move here?

▶ Do you know anyone who has recently immigrated to America? [Maybe from their church, doctor's office, or restaurant they frequent.] Are the immigrants you know negatively or positively influencing our community?

▶ You know, my friend [immigrant's name] is an immigrant. Their story has impacted me. [Share their story.]

America's founding documents were inspired by God. Some American Christian nationalists will say America's founding documents were inspired by God. Other versions of this sentiment include the idea that the founding documents are holy or given to us by God.[34] The *inspiration of Scripture* is a theological term that comes from 2 Timothy 3:16. It refers to the belief that God divinely guided the formation of the Bible, which often implies that it is sacred and authoritative in a unique way.

The rhetoric works to treat America's Declaration of Independence and Constitution as sacred texts, specially ordained by God. While these documents make some reference to the divine, they were also heavily influenced by European Enlightenment philosophers like Jean-Jacques Rousseau and John Locke.[35]

Coaching notes. Many American Christian nationalists have a high view of Scripture and a high view of America's founding documents. In conversations with our mission field we want to honor both but also show that the documents formed by the founders are not on par with Holy Scripture. Moreover, the actual text of the Declaration of Independence and the Constitution refer more to human actions than divine actions. While they are not devoid of references to God, they are substantially human-centered documents.

When engaging in conversations on this topic, we can guide people to spend time reading the texts together and invite them to share what they notice. It can be especially helpful to ask how they think these texts use or elevate uniquely Christian teachings, such as the divinity of Jesus, the Trinity, or the indwelling Holy Spirit, none of which are mentioned in either document.

Clarifying questions

- ▶ What does *inspired by God* mean to you?

- ▶ Is this divine inspiration unique to America's founding documents? Are other countries' documents inspired by God as well?

Possible shared values

- ▶ God is sovereign over all of history. Nothing happens apart from him.

► God loves the people of America (though not uniquely).

► America's founders were very wise in how they set up the government.

Shibboleths

► I believe God has blessed America in many ways.

► I can see that many of the founding fathers were influenced by Christianity and incorporated some of their beliefs into the founding documents.

Red flags

► America is designed to be a secular country. Leave God out of it.

► The founders were all deists or agnostics.

Good things to honor

► I am thankful for the rights and liberties inscribed in the founding documents.

► I believe that God is powerful over human history and establishes governments for good.

► There is much in the founding documents that align with the teachings of Scripture.

Humble subversion

► I am so glad that you love America. I do too! Maybe we could read the founding documents together. Let's notice how they talk about God, Jesus, the Holy Spirit, and the Bible.[36] Do you think these documents elevate God's actions or human actions in the founding of America? We can see that there are amendments to the Constitution. Let's read those together. What do you notice?

▷ Do you believe these amendments are inspired by God as well?

▷ If these documents were inspired by God, why did they need amending?

- ▶ Are there any portions of Scripture that imply government documents like these are to be viewed as sacred?

- ▶ I hear a lot of people saying that the founding documents were divinely inspired. The Bible shows government leaders claiming to have divine endorsement and then doing ungodly things. An example of this can be found in 1 Kings 22. How do you think the claim that the documents were divinely inspired could be used by corrupt people to justify evil actions?

Democrats are demonic. While American Christian nationalism is not inherently Republican (see "Christian Nationalism Is Not Christian Conservatism" in chapter 2), some have used the dehumanizing title *DEMONcrat* to speak of those aligned with the Democratic Party.[37] Modern American Christian nationalists have ramped up this dehumanizing rhetoric, often invoking biblical language to equate political progressives with demons, evil spirits, or the antichrist and accusing them of participating in activities like child sacrifice, pedophilia, Satan worship, and blood rituals.[38]

Coaching notes. One of our goals in conversations related to this statement is to humanize the *other*. While many American Christian nationalists will point to a few policies held by many Democrats (usually related to abortion, marriage, and sexuality), we can help to show that there are many faithful Christians who prefer the Democratic Party because it aligns more closely with their understanding of the teachings of Scripture.[39] The following statements can help to add nuance and remind our hearers that those who are not aligned with us politically are still people made in God's image and likely have healthy, wise reasons for voting the way they do.

In America one of the best ways to do this is by exploring the witness of Black Christians in America, 84 percent of whom prefer the Democratic Party.[40]

Clarifying questions

- ▶ Are you talking about the Democratic leadership or the people who vote for them?

- Do you know any Democrats personally? If so, tell me about them.
- What do you think Democrats believe?

Possible shared values

- Voting should be based on core values, not just allegiance to a party.
- We should show discernment when voting for candidates for public office.
- There are some things about the Democratic platform that concern me.

Shibboleths

- I believe Christians should vote for candidates who are more likely to lead in a way that honors the teaching of Jesus.
- I also want our government to have policies that honor God and are aligned with the teachings of Jesus.

Red flags

- Republicans are also demonic.
- Republicans are racist, fascist nazis.
- Democrats are more Christian than Republicans.

Good things to honor

- Wanting to honor God with how we vote and who we vote for.
- Having government leaders who seek to honor God and lead in ways that bend toward the teaching of Scripture.

Humble subversion

- The Bible talks a lot about caring for widows, immigrants, the poor, and orphans. I wonder how many Christians vote for Democrats because they believe that their policies are more in line with these biblical principles. What do you think?
- Why do you think such a high percentage of Black and Brown Christians vote for Democratic candidates? How might their story impact our thinking on the matter?

► Scripture says that the devil presents as an angel of light (2 Corinthians 11:14), giving the impression it is righteous when in fact it is evil. Do you think that there could be an evil influence in the Republican Party too?

CONSPIRACY THEORIES AND OPPRESSION NARRATIVES

Christians are under attack in America. This is a pure expression of the persecution complex referred to in chapter three.[41] It captures the deep anxiety of ethnic erasure that many in our mission field experience daily. Notice the violence inherent in the statement "under attack." This is battlefield language and promotes the idea that we are under imminent threat of destruction.

Coaching notes. American Christian nationalists are frequently being told they are under attack because of their beliefs. Many evangelical movements and organizations in America argue that Christians in America are being persecuted because of their faith. While religious persecution is certainly a threat (especially in some parts of the world more than others), most of what American Christian nationalists experience is the result of living in a pluralistic culture, such as the clerk using "Happy Holidays" instead of "Merry Christmas" or the "Coexist" bumper sticker composed of icons from various faith traditions.

I invite you to encourage your conversation partners to explore the nature of true persecution and to examine how the teachings and example of Jesus shape our response to resistance and persecution.

Clarifying questions

► In what ways are you seeing this play out?

► Are there specific things that Christians are doing that instigate the persecution you are seeing?

► How do we discern persecution from the consequences of being combative or hypocritical?

Possible shared values

► Being persecuted for one's religious beliefs is unjust.

- ▶ In a pluralistic society like America there should be no persecution or resistance to any religious expression.

Shibboleths

- ▶ I believe Christians should be able to practice their faith without fear of persecution.

- ▶ It saddens me to know that people experience resistance for following the way of Jesus.

- ▶ I know that many cultures, governments, and leaders around the world are resistant to Christians and often work against the cause of Christ.

Red flags

- ▶ You are being too sensitive about this.

- ▶ There is no war on Christianity (or Christmas).

- ▶ Christmas-less coffee cups are not persecution.

Good things to honor

- ▶ All people should be free to practice their religious traditions peacefully without fear of physical harm or other forms of persecution.

- ▶ It is good for Christians to practice their faith in the public sphere.

Humble subversion

- ▶ As I read the Scriptures it seems like Christians should expect resistance for following the way of Jesus. Let's read 1 Peter 2:11-17 together. Why do you think Peter wrote these words? How might they shape our understanding of the pushback we experience today?

- ▶ I have seen many Christian public figures use dehumanizing and harmful language to talk about people in the LGBTQ+ community. I wonder if some of the resistance Christians feel is because of a lack of compassion and mercy from these figureheads. What do you think?

▶ Certainly, there are those within our country who don't approve of Christianity, but it seems to me that some of the resistance comes when Christians behave in ways that are not like Jesus. How do you think this hypocrisy factors into the criticisms of Christianity?

▶ I have been thinking recently about the many passages in the New Testament that talk about how the church should be marked by qualities like love, joy, peace, patience, and kindness, and I sometimes wonder if we were better at living this out, would we face so much resistance from our neighbors? What do you think?

The election was stolen. In recent years there has been a significant increase in claims that elections across the United States have been rigged, often arising after closely contested election outcomes. Many American Christian nationalists claim that clandestine groups are hiding in the shadows orchestrating massive fraud to elect liberal candidates. Some have even claimed that a certain election was rigged before the voting process was over.

Coaching notes. Remember that many of the people in our mission field are inundated with curated propaganda from national news outlets, conferences, rallies, social media platforms, and news radio. The information they receive is constantly reinforced by the members of the American Christian nationalist community. They are extremely suspicious of any government official, news outlet, or media personality that provides conflicting data, often referring to it as fake news.

While thus far there has been little to no evidence of election tampering across America, it will likely do no good to argue the merits of the case. Instead, I encourage you to guide the conversation toward shared values (elections in the United States should be free and fair) and acknowledge that people in power will often use their influence to garner more power, often using any means necessary. We see this play out in Scripture and all of human history. While you may not believe that *this* election was rigged, it is certainly within the realm of possibility for people to commit such evil. It is not uncommon for powerful people to violate the law in ways that disenfranchise those who have less influence. In your conversations with our mission field I suggest focusing on the reality that there are people who wish to do evil and then guiding them to Jesus, asking how his teachings and example show us how to respond to those who would commit transgressions in the world.

Clarifying questions

► Which election(s) are you referring to?

► Is this different from other elections you've witnessed in the past?

► What are the protections we have in place to promote or ensure free and fair elections?

Possible shared values

► A healthy democratic process allows everyone's voice to be heard, especially those without much power and influence.

► Truth, fairness, and justice are good things.

Shibboleths

► I think election integrity is critically important for a healthy democracy.

► I think everyone's vote should count.

► The democratic process is a precious gift. We should work to ensure it is healthy and continues for future generations.

Red flags

► There is no way the election could be rigged.

► The people making this claim are sore losers.

Good things to honor

► I believe that our elections should be fair and just and that everyone's vote should count.

► I believe that the people overseeing our election process should have integrity and should be accountable for their work.

Humble subversion

- ► I am so glad that you care about this issue. I do too! I have also heard claims that the election was rigged. How can we tell if these claims are valid? What tools or systems can we use to make these determinations?

- ► Let's say that an election was stolen. How does Jesus inform our response? I don't think he would encourage us to take up arms and violently overthrow those we perceive as enemies. If that is not the answer, what should we do?

- ► Perhaps Jesus would call us to serve in our local community. What do you think are some life-giving ways that we can work with election officials in our area? Are there ways we can encourage them and support them in their work?

Billionaire puppet masters are controlling the world. This statement has many forms and is usually about a secret cabal of powerful elites who are conspiring to pull the strings of power within America and even the world. Often, these evil overlords are portrayed as globalist antichrist figures, closet socialists, and even sadistic pedophiles. American Christian nationalist leaders often invoke this imagery, claiming that this secret power bloc is using its resources to bribe, extort, and control career politicians (usually only Democrats) and the liberal deep state. The oft-repeated MAGA rallying cry "Drain the Swamp!" stems from this belief.

Coaching notes. While the statement sounds like the plot of a 1980s thriller movie, the instinct is not far off from the teaching of Scripture. Throughout the Bible we find warnings that those with money and power are often marked by injustice and corruption as they strive to gain more influence and wealth. While our conversation partners may misdiagnose these evildoers' identities and the extent of their guilt, we must not dismiss the reality that people in power often perpetrate evil acts.

In our conversations we want to shift from focusing on the wrongdoers to thinking about how Jesus shapes our perspective and interactions with those who do evil. We can help them think through how Jesus' teachings influence our responses and where we can put our trust. We can remind them that Jesus is the Lord of all and that the power of the cross disarms the power of the sword and all who would wield it. We can be a people of peace, resting in the knowledge that God is in control. The goal here is normalizing the reality of powerful people doing evil and then pointing to the more powerful Jesus, so we can rest knowing that the overlords are not ultimately in control.

Clarifying questions

- ► Tell me why this matters to you.
- ► How are you seeing this take place in America?
- ► Are there specific people you are thinking of?

Possible shared values

- ► I want the people leading us to have integrity and to do good. When leaders lead with evil intent or evil methods, people get hurt.
- ► Powerful people who do evil should be held accountable.

Shibboleths

- ► I think there are a lot of leaders who engage in evil acts and lead in ways that are contrary to the teaching and example of Jesus.
- ► The Scriptures often teach about the corrupting nature of greed.
- ► Greed and lust for power can corrupt leaders who will often do acts of injustice to gain more power and wealth.

Red flags

- ► People who believe in evil billionaires are just jealous.
- ► That's merely a conspiracy theory.

Good things to honor

- ► I want our rulers to be just, compassionate, honor others, and focus on serving the people they lead instead of lining their own pockets.
- ► I am concerned about the integrity of those who lead.

Humble subversion

▶ Let's suppose that there are people secretly operating within the halls of power, pulling the strings. Like Pharaoh or Caesar in the Bible, they leverage worldly power to promote evil ends. It seems like this is something that could always be happening. The book of Revelation seems to show that there are always powers at work in the kingdoms of this world that will give their allegiance to anything that gets them more strength. How do you think Jesus would have us respond in situations like this?

▶ Lately, I've been thinking about what the Bible says about power in this world. In Matthew 20:25 Jesus says that the leaders of this world lord their power over their subjects, seemingly in ways that are harmful to those they lead. In Ephesians 6 the apostle Paul says that there are evil powers at work in the world. The book of Revelation seems to agree with Paul's perspective that there are dark forces at work in the world and that leaders often tether themselves to that power. I have been thinking a lot about how the teachings of Jesus guide me in how to live in this kind of world, seeking peace, grace, mercy, and longsuffering. What do you think Jesus might say to us today?

▶ I too am very concerned about people using power in corrupt, unjust ways. I am also concerned that some of those people are doing and saying things that I like. How can we protect ourselves from being seduced by their false promises?

Prayer and Bibles are outlawed in schools. In recent years American Christian nationalists have referred to schools as the front line of the culture wars.[42] They compel their adherents to attend school board meetings to raise contentious issues, call for the expulsion of woke teachers, and ban books that they believe promote ideas that will negatively influence children.[43] They also frequently advocate for those in their ranks to secure positions of power within the governing bodies that oversee local public schools, often advocating for policies that would reinstate public prayer and mandatory Bible study.[44]

Coaching notes. This bold assertion is patently false and bears false witness against public schools in America. Both Bibles and prayer are legally allowed in public schools as evidenced by modern movements like Focus on the Family's "Bring Your Bible to School Day" and the "See You at the Pole" prayer initiative.[45] While prayer and Bible reading are legal, we'll want to explore expectations of public schooling relating to religion. Is compulsory Bible reading and prayer good for kids? Who gets to decide the prayers and Bible translations?

When engaging in conversations about schools, it is good to remember that they are not monolithic; they are run by local governments as diverse as their community. What is true for a school in Boston may not be true for a school in Miami.[46] Remember that our American Christian nationalist neighbors are often receiving curated propaganda about public schools from national media outlets, not from the schools themselves. We can work to build credibility by sharing our concerns about public schooling while encouraging people to be lovingly involved at the local level; we can be informed with firsthand engagement and explore ways to engage our school districts with a posture of service. And so we'll want to invite our conversation partners to look closer to home, sharing stories of our church's youth engaging in clubs (like Young Life) on campus and the good work God is doing in the lives of those serving in and attending public schools. Also if there are any teachers or administrators in your church, I encourage you to take them out for a meal, hear their stories, and advocate for them and their work.

Clarifying questions

► Where are you seeing this?

► Is this happening in our school district?

► Which prayers and Scripture are outlawed? Is it all religions and denominations or just evangelical Christians?

Possible shared values

► I believe that kids should be able to express their faith without fear of reprimand, bigotry, or hate.

▶ I value the Bible and think that people would benefit from studying it.

Shibboleths

▶ The Bible is the Word of God. It is good for kids to know the Bible and to pray if they want to.

▶ I believe that healthy, honest, truth-telling schooling is important for developing future generations.

▶ Schools should empower children to live with virtue and integrity.

Red flags

▶ Religion has no place in public schools. No one should talk with kids about religion.

▶ Schools should be able to teach whatever they want.

Good things to honor

▶ I love that you want kids to have the freedom to study the Bible and pray if they want to.

▶ I know you value prayer and want everyone to have the freedom to pray in whatever way they desire.

Humble subversion

▶ I love that you want kids to know the Jesus of the Bible. However, given the variety of views on prayer and Scripture in the Christian tradition (much less other religious traditions), I wonder if it is wise for us to ask our educators to navigate these complexities. Would we want teachers to give priority to a specific Bible translation or form of prayer? Is it wise and loving to ask a Catholic teacher to lead the children in an Anglican prayer? Should we mandate that an Armenian Orthodox principal lead the school in a Wesleyan reading of Scripture? What do you think?

▶ How do you think kids who don't pray the same way would feel if their leaders at school led them in a prayer that was different from what they did at home or in their church?

▸ How might the students from other religious traditions feel if their teachers promoted a faith different from theirs? Might that create animosity within the students?

▸ Deuteronomy 6 shows that the family and faith community bear the responsibility to teach children how to live out their faith. How do you think we can prioritize the family's convictions and responsibility and allow for prayer and Scripture engagement in our schools?

NOW YOU DO IT! CREATE YOUR OWN FIELD GUIDE

The preceding pages have served as sample conversations you can have with your American Christian nationalist neighbors. However, these have primarily come from my context. What are the phrases you are hearing? Use this template to create your plan for loving, humbly subversive conversations.

CREATE YOUR OWN FIELD GUIDE

STATEMENT

Write a statement you've heard from your American Christian nationalist neighbors.

_____

_____

_____

CLARIFYING QUESTIONS

What neutral questions could you ask that would deepen your understanding of their perspective?

_____

_____

_____

POSSIBLE SHARED VALUES

What are some of the values underneath the statement that you likely share?

_____

_____

_____

SHIBBOLETHS

What are some words or phrases you could use in good faith that would communicate that you are a friend?

_____

_____

_____

RED FLAGS

What words or phrases might communicate that you are an "enemy"?

_____

_____

_____

GOOD THINGS TO HONOR

What are some of the good things connected to the statement that you can honor during your conversations?

_____

_____

_____

HUMBLE SUBVERSION

What are some questions or responses you can weave into the conversation that could gently invite your conversation partner(s) to join you in thinking deeper about this issue? Are there portions of Scripture that would be good to explore together that might speak to the statement?

_____

_____

_____

PROACTIVE EXERCISES

So far, we have focused on responding to statements made by those in our mission field. This section will explore some helpful, proactive exercises that can expose our mission field to new ways of thinking and invite them to join us in thoughtful conversations about perspectives contrary to American Christian nationalism.

These exercises are designed to take place in the context of a hospitable environment in which all parties feel safe to be their authentic selves and share their perspectives without fear of abandonment or ridicule. Remember that while many conversations start with the *head* (facts and opinions), we want to steer the conversation to the *heart* (feelings and needs).

Political commitment inventory. Most American Christian nationalist organizations do not provide thoughtful reasons for their preferred political positions or encourage critical engagement with the ideas they promote. Thus, many in our mission field hold to political commitments they have borrowed from their favorite leaders.

To help those in our mission field discern their convictions about specific political issues, ask them to join you in taking a political commitment inventory.

Take a blank piece of paper and write on it your currently held political commitments, one per line, and invite your friend to do the same. Next to each commitment, each of you should gauge how deeply you are committed to the belief. Is this an opinion? A preference? A spiritual conviction?

Take time to discuss each of the commitments, explore why this commitment is essential to them, and share yours as well. As a final step take each commitment line by line and ask, How might Jesus want to shape or reshape my thinking on this commitment? A critical component of this exercise is to be open to changing your convictions too! The Spirit of the living God is working on all of us!

Media fast. Have you ever fasted from something? It is a frequent practice in many parts of the world to fast for a season or do a cleanse in which a person, desiring to be healthier, abstains from certain food or drinks they believe could be harming their bodies.

Much of the anxiety and outrage that burns within our mission field is mercilessly stoked by various media outlets that spew a steady stream of incendiary fearmongering under the guise of news. By simply refusing to engage in that material for a period of time, you may see lower blood pressure, less rage in conversations with loved ones, and perhaps even a more peaceful thought life. You might approach someone in your mission field and say, "You know, I notice my blood pressure is high whenever I listen to cable news or doom-scroll X (the former Twitter). I am more angry, anxious, and fearful. I also notice I spend multiple hours a week filling my mind and heart with stuff I can't change. Would you join me in a two-week media fast? We can check in daily and see if it is positively affecting our lives."

During the fast, check in to see how your friend is feeling. Are they noticing anything different about their daily life, conversations, and overall sense of self? What did they notice? Did they spend more time doing things they valued? Was there more time to enjoy the people they love? After the fast, debrief on how you can both change your media intake for a healthier lifestyle in the future.

Book studies. Studying a book together can be a terrific way to engage ideas without bringing them up yourself. As a reading partner you can take a passive role in raising issues (let the book do that) and instead focus on listening and encouraging deeper thought and prayer.

Studying books that explore political issues can be perilous, especially if they include red-flag language that communicates the author is an enemy (see "Shibboleths and red flags" in chapter 5). The following books by Christian political thinkers are recommended for their excellent content and thoughtful rhetoric, which I believe will be more likely to be graciously received by those in our mission field.

► *The Political Disciple: A Theology of Public Life* by Vincent Bacote

► *How to Be a Patriotic Christian: Love of Country as Love of Neighbor* by Richard Mouw

► *The Liturgy of Politics* by Kaitlyn Schiess

► *The Search for Christian America* by Mark Noll, George Marsden, and Nathan Hatch

► *The Need to Be Whole: Patriotism and the History of Prejudice* by Wendell Berry

For an expanded list of recommended book studies, visit the Disarming Leviathan website (https://disarmingleviathan.com).

Bible studies. For those in our mission field with a high view of Scripture, there is nothing better than a good old-fashioned Bible study. I recommend these three studies be done in sequential order.

The kingdom of God. Jesus came proclaiming the gospel of the kingdom of God, a kingdom that does not operate according to this world's systems. This is good news for everyone and involves a radical new way of living *on earth as it is in heaven*. This study explores relevant portions of Scripture to give you a deeper understanding of the kingdom of God and how we can live as faithful citizens today.

Biblical patriotism. Scripture is full of examples of people striving to live out their faith in politically charged environments. Figures like

Daniel, Esther, Paul, and others can guide us in living as ambassadors of God's kingdom and simultaneously love our fellow Americans as ourselves. This study will equip readers with a better understanding of how to love our country without worshiping it.

Quartet of the vulnerable. Throughout Scripture the needs of widows, the poor, immigrants, and orphans are frequently elevated as a primary concern of God and his followers. This study examines the multitude of relevant texts and will equip you to discern your convictions on how the Scriptures shape our understanding and give us the wisdom to meet the needs of those on the margins. For these and other recommended studies, visit the Disarming Leviathan website (https://disarmingleviathan.com).

Thirty days of prayer. Many within our mission field say they believe in the power of prayer. We can invite them to join us for intentional times of prayer that focus on specific issues we believe are important. For instance, you could commit to dedicating the next thirty days to praying together in person or on the phone through a curated list of issues. For a recommended list of prayer topics visit the Disarming Leviathan website (https://disarmingleviathan.com). During these times of prayer, consider inviting God to shape you into the type of people who display the values of the kingdom of God in your interactions with people you disagree with.

8

LEVIATHAN'S END

A Story of Hope

In that day, the LORD will punish with his
sword—his fierce, great and powerful sword—
Leviathan the gliding serpent, Leviathan the coiling
serpent; he will slay the monster of the sea.

ISAIAH 71:1

IS THERE ANY HOPE? I hear that question a lot in my encounters with people like you and me seeking to reach our mission field. Leviathan is so powerful and seductive that redemption can sometimes seem impossible, especially when so many of those we love are so deeply entrenched in American Christian nationalism. It almost feels like change is unattainable. They are too far gone.

Moreover, many of us may feel uncertain, too weak, or ill-equipped to stand against the power of the dragon. The tools of hospitality and humble subversion can feel puny compared to the dominating might of Leviathan.

I know the feeling.

But remember, our job is not to defeat Leviathan. That's God's job. Our role is to use the methods of Jesus to reach the people he loves and seek to restore them with a gentle spirit. Sadly, there will be some, perhaps even many, who will not choose to turn and follow the way of Jesus. If I understand the Scriptures correctly, there will be many who choose to listen to leaders who say the things they want to hear and follow them all the way to the grave (see 2 Timothy 4:3).

We cannot slay the great dragon of American Christian nationalism, but we can compassionately care for the souls of the people caught up in it and seek to restore them to a flourishing relationship with Jesus and his church. While some may never change, our faithfulness might plant a seed in their hearts that will grow into the fruit of repentance. We cannot see the end, but we can be faithful in the moments we are given.

I began this book by noticing that 2020 was an apocalypse, a revelation of the fractures that were hidden beneath the surface. It is perhaps fitting then to conclude this book by looking at the greatest apocalypse, the one at the end of your Bible known as Revelation.

Revelation was written to followers of Jesus living under the oppressive Roman Empire. Just like today, people at that time were tempted by the enticing power of the empire's promise of political influence, military power, and financial gain. They felt the pressure to conform to religious fundamentalism, ethnic supremacy, and fearmongering (Acts 6). For many of the original hearers of Revelation, following Jesus was costing them family relationships, financial opportunities, and even their lives. The book acknowledges Leviathan's power (seen in the characters of the beast and the dragon) to deceive and seduce people by promising economic and political gain. The merchants and kings of the earth are said to have given themselves to the power of the beast (Revelation 18).

While the evil creature is mighty, the faithful are kept safe by the power of Jesus, known as the Lamb. Against all human expectations, Leviathan is subdued, not by human domination, not by the might of the sword, but by the self-sacrificial power of the Lamb of God.

The slain-then-resurrected Lamb of God, Jesus, God in the flesh, conquers evil and death and reunites heaven and earth, establishing an eternal Eden-like kingdom where all the peoples of the world live in harmony, peace, and justice.

You and I live between the resurrection and the time of the final victory of the Lamb. In this in-between-time we are called to live in light of Jesus' ultimate victory, to hope in his redemptive power, and to trust that one day he will restore all that is broken. This is not an alternative way to fight the culture wars. It is refusing to fight the war altogether, to lay down the way of the sword, and to pick up the way of the cross. This is the way that ultimately leads to redemption, restoration, and complete victory over evil.

Our hope for the future victory of Jesus means that faithfulness to Jesus today is never in vain. The Spirit of the living God is active, moving in our midst. Jesus longs to reconcile and restore everyone to a right relationship with him, including American Christian nationalists.

The resurrected Christ has defeated death and will one day subdue Leviathan. Though some days it may not seem likely, Jesus *will* win, and he will redeem and restore all that is broken. By the power of the Spirit that redemptive, restorative work can break into the lives of the people in our mission field now! Consider the apostle Paul. When we first hear about Paul in the book of Acts, he is referred to as Saul.

Saul was religiously devout and extremely zealous for his nation, Israel. As a Pharisee he was deeply devoted to protecting and promoting the traditions and customs of his people. Blinded by his convictions, he saw the people who followed Jesus as a threat to the things he held dear. He was so committed to his cause that he endorsed mob violence, threats, persecution, and even murder of those he viewed as his enemy (Acts 7:54–8:1).

One day, while traveling to Damascus to snuff out the church there, a blinding light enveloped him. He fell to the ground and heard a voice saying, "Saul, Saul, why do you persecute me?" (Acts 9:4).

In that moment Jesus radically transformed Saul's heart. Saul experienced repentance, a *metanoia* moment, a mind-renewing, life-altering experience.

Then Jesus sent Ananias to minister to Saul, who was welcomed into the local church. Eventually, Saul became a servant of Christ, dedicating his life to sharing the good news of Jesus with as many nations as he could.

Saul's conversion became a beacon of hope for many and a testament to the redemptive power of the living God who can transform even the hardest of hearts. Saul's story reminds us that redemption is always possible, even for those who are currently in Leviathan's grasp.

If Christ is raised from the dead, there is hope. If he transformed Saul, he can redeem and restore those we love. As we work to point them to Jesus, we can rest knowing that ultimately the work of repentance is not something we can accomplish in our own power. That is God's job. Our role is to be faithful in the opportunities that he gives to us.

He is faithful to deliver and faithful to restore.

Our hope rests not in our arguments or techniques. Our hope rests in nothing but the power of Jesus, who loves our mission field more than we can ever imagine.

Many years after his restoration Saul, who often goes by his Roman name, Paul, launched new churches all around the Roman world. He wrote a letter to Christians living in a city called Philippi to encourage them. They were feeling the tension of faithfully following Jesus while facing intense opposition. He writes, "Let your gentleness be evident to all. *The Lord is near. Do not be anxious* about anything, but in every situation, by prayer and petition, with thanksgiving, present your requests to God. And the peace of God, which transcends all understanding, will guard your hearts and minds in Christ Jesus" (Philippians 4:5-8).

I love this text. He addresses the anxiety and fear the Philippian Christians were feeling with a powerful truth: *the Lord is near.*

As you set out to missionally engage American Christian nationalists, remember, Jesus is nearer to you than you are to yourself. He knows firsthand what it is like to lose friends who turn away and pursue the power of this world. He also holds the universe together and is faithful to fulfill his promises to us.

I invite you to move forward into this mission work, in prayer and thanksgiving, knowing that Jesus cares for you, will guard you, and will bring peace to your weary heart.

Jesus loves you so much!

ACKNOWLEDGMENTS

I AM SO THANKFUL FOR the many friends God has placed in my life. Their encouragement and prayer have been such a gift. I am grateful to Rick Efird, Phil Herndon, Brandon O'Brien, Teena Dare, Brad Vaughn, John DelHousaye, Charlie Meo, and Don Allen for their wisdom and assistance in the formation of this project. I especially want to thank Monika Morris for spending countless hours helping me put words to ideas and bringing order to the disordered mess that is my brain. Without her, this project would not have come to fruition.

I am also thankful for the network of pastors and ministry leaders who are working to engage American Christian nationalism in our churches and communities. This type of work can be extremely painful, but it is made easier with good friends who help carry the burden.

Finally, thanks to my wife and children, who made countless sacrifices during the formation of this book. I love you very much.

NOTES

1. THE APOCALYPSE

[1]John Burnett, "Americans Are Fleeing to Places Where Political Views Match Their Own," NPR, February 18, 2022, www.npr.org/2022/02/18/1081295373/the-big -sort-americans-move-to-areas-political-alignment.

[2]Eric Ortlund, *Piercing Leviathan: God's Defeat of Evil in the Book of Job*, New Studies in Biblical Theology 56 (Downers Grove, IL: InterVarsity Press, 2021), 4.

[3]For a helpful overview of critical race theory, complete with links to many good resources, check out this four-part series: Sitara Roden, "Voices with Ed Stetzer: Framing Critical Race Theory, Part 1," *ChurchLeaders*, September 2, 2021, https:// churchleaders.com/pastors/404441-ed-stetzer-framing-critical-race-theory -part-1.html.

[4]Peter Stone, "Money and Misinformation: How Turning Point USA Became a Formidable Pro-Trump Force," *Guardian*, October 23, 2021, www.theguardian.com /us-news/2021/oct/23/turning-point-rightwing-youth-group-critics-tactics; Matthew Boedy, "Ten Years of Turning Point USA," *Political Research Associates*, January 28, 2022, https://politicalresearch.org/2022/01/28/ten-years-turning -point-usa.

[5]Russell Moore, "Christian Nationalism Cannot Save the World," *Christianity Today*, September 29, 2022, www.christianitytoday.com/ct/2022/september -web-only/christian-nationalism-cannot-save-world-politics-elections.html.

2. A FIGURE IN THE SHADOWS

[1]For more on the role of Christian nationalism and the insurrection of January 6, see Samuel Perry and Andrew L. Whitehead, "The Role of Christian Nationalism on January 6 and After: What National Survey Data Tell Us," *SocArXiv*, March 2023, doi:10.31235/osf.io/qu5h6.

[2]Marjorie Taylor Greene, "I'm a God-Fearing Christian. I Love Our Country and Its People. This Is Why I'm a Proud Christian Nationalist," Instagram, July 26, 2022, www.instagram.com/p/CgfyNqpNjbb.

[3]"Understanding the Threat of White Christian Nationalism to American Democracy Today," *Brookings*, February 17, 2023, www.brookings.edu/events /understanding-the-threat-of-white-christian-nationalism-to-american -democracy-today.

[4]"Google Books Ngram Viewer—Google Product," accessed May 1, 2023, https:// books.google.com/ngrams/graph?content=Christian+Nationalism&year_start =1800&year_end=2019&corpus=en-2019&smoothing=3.

[5]Tim Dickinson, "MAGA Pastor Says Christians Must 'Be the Ones Writing Laws,'" *Rolling Stone*, accessed May 24, 2023, www.rollingstone.com/politics/politics -features/maga-pastor-sean-feucht-trump-christian-nationalism-1234721527.

[6]James Silberman and Dusty Deevers, "The Statement on Christian Nationalism and the Gospel," May 21, 2023, www.statementonchristiannationalism.com.

[7]People belonging to Jesus are first called Christians in Acts 11. The term is only used a few times in Scripture.

[8]Matthew W. Bates, *Salvation by Allegiance Alone: Rethinking Faith, Works, and the Gospel of Jesus the King* (Grand Rapids, MI: Baker Academic, 2017).

[9]Elias Joseph Bickerman, *Studies in Jewish and Christian History*, Ancient Judaism & Early Christianity (Boston: Brill, 2007), 803.

[10]David T. Koyzis, *Political Visions and Illusions: A Survey & Christian Critique of Contemporary Ideologies* (Downers Grove, IL: InterVarsity Press, 2019), 91.

[11]Koyzis, *Political Visions and Illusions*, 91.

[12]Bernard R. Crick, *In Defence of Politics* (Chicago: University of Chicago Press, 1992), 75. "It is notorious that no single objective criterion of the national unit has ever been found."

[13]David Goodblatt, *Elements of Ancient Jewish Nationalism* (New York: Cambridge University Press, 2006), 6.

[14]Notice that these cultural expressions are not static. They evolve over time, frequently reshaped by new generations. They also change as they interact with other cultures. Many in the culinary arts use the word fusion to describe this phenomenon. However, over time, the fusion simply becomes a new cultural expression of a particular nation.

[15]Colin Woodard, *American Nations: A History of the Eleven Rival Regional Cultures of North America* (New York: Penguin, 2012), 3.

[16]Stephen R Covey, *The Seven Habits of Highly Effective People: Restoring the Character Ethic* (New York: Free Press, 2004), 237.

[17]This does depend on which years one is looking at. For instance, there seems to be a significant increase after the Great Awakening and other movements. See Roger Finke and Rodney Stark, *The Churching of America, 1776–2005:*

Winners and Losers in Our Religious Economy (Chicago: Rutgers University Press, 2005).

[18]Mark A. Noll, Nathan O. Hatch, and George M. Marsden, *The Search for Christian America* (Colorado Springs, CO: Helmers & Howard, 1989), 19.

[19]You can find a copy at "Declaration of Independence," National Archives, accessed October 30, 2023, www.archives.gov/founding-docs/declaration-transcript.

[20]Mark David Hall, "Did America Have a Christian Founding?" Heritage Foundation, June 7, 2011, www.heritage.org/political-process/report/did-america -have-christian-founding.

[21]Noll, Hatch, and Marsden, *Search for Christian America,* 131.

[22]"Because the institutional approval of [the] church . . . the Nazi state was expressed so openly and never recanted, I believe that approval is the primary impression Germans at the time would have perceived. When ordinary Germans, including church members . . . were asked to do horrific things by the Nazi state, they presumably had a right to think they were given permission by their pastors. . . . Hitler had been praised as God's gift to Germany." Robert P. Ericksen, *Complicity in the Holocaust: Churches and Universities in Nazi Germany* (Cambridge: Cambridge University Press, 2012), xvi.

[23]Jeanne Whalen, "Russian Orthodox Leader Backs War in Ukraine, Divides Faith." *Washington Post,* accessed April 21, 2022, www.washingtonpost.com/world /2022/04/18/russian-orthodox-church-ukraine-war.

[24]Finke and Stark, *Churching of America,* loc. 96.

[25]C. S. Lewis, *The Four Loves* (New York: Houghton Mifflin Harcourt, 1991), 29.

[26]See "Understanding the Threat of White Christian Nationalism to American Democracy Today," and the work of journalists Katherine Steward, Jack Jenkins, Bob Smietana, Richard Ruelas, Angela Denker, Sam Perry, Andrew Whitehead, and Philip Gorsky, and organizations like Religion News Service, *Christianity Today,* and *The Atlantic.*

[27]Paul D. Miller, "What Is Christian Nationalism?" *Christianity Today,* February 3, 2021, www.christianitytoday.com/ct/2021/february-web-only/what-is-christian -nationalism.html.

[28]Jemar Tisby, "A Conversation About Christian Nationalism on NPR's 1A," Footnotes by Jemar Tisby substack, July 12, 2022, https://jemartisby.substack.com /p/icymi-a-conversation-about-christian.

[29]Keller makes this point in his books *Counterfeit Gods* and *Every Good Endeavor,* and many of his sermons (see https://gospelinlife.com). Keller is one of the greatest influences on my pastoral vocation and devotional life. He passed away the day before I wrote this note. I struggle to put into words his meaning in my life and simply commend his work to you.

[30]Michael Frost, *Keep Christianity Weird: Embracing the Discipline of Being Different* (Colorado Springs, CO: NavPress, 2018), 17.

[31]"Christian Nationalist Rhetoric & Identity Formation w/ Matthew Boedy," *Disarming Leviathan* (podcast), June 22, 2023, https://disarmingleviathan.com/podcast/christian-nationalist-rhetoric-identity-formation-interview-with-matthew-boedy.

[32]Throughout this book the term *American Christian nationalism* is used to describe a phenomenon that some scholars refer to as White Christian nationalism. While I agree with many of their observations about how White supremacy has shaped this movement, those in our mission field recoil at the claim that racism is part of their movement. However, I recognize that the majority of those advocating for Christian nationalism in America are White. See Samuel Perry and Andrew L. Whitehead, "The Role of Christian Nationalism on January 6 and After: What National Survey Data Tell Us," SocArXiv, March 23, 2023, doi:10.31235/osf.io/qu5h6.

[33]Philip S. Gorski, *The Flag and the Cross: White Christian Nationalism and the Threat to American Democracy* (New York: Oxford University Press, 2022), 4.

[34]Nilay Saiya, "Christian Nationalism's Threat to Global Democracy," Review of Faith & International Affairs, May 12, 2023, doi:10.1080/15570274.2023.2204679.

[35]"The pattern that Democrats and Independents have become more Christian nationalist since 2016 is surely NOT what anyone would expect to see during this time period. And, it is important to keep the relative levels of CN views within these groups in perspective. Still, the patterns are consistent with the uptick in Christian persecution rhetoric that was widespread throughout the past fifteen years (i.e., during Obama's presidency, and especially during Trump's).

"This pattern indicates that many Democrats are cross-pressured by a CN world-view, suggesting it could be an effective strategy for Republicans and a difficult one for Democrats to counter. It also highlights that we can't make simple assumptions about party identifiers—reducing claims to 'Democrats are the party of diversity and tolerance, opposed to Christian nationalism.'" Paul A. Djupe, Andrew R. Lewis, and Anand E. Sokhey, *The Full Armor of God* (Cambridge: Cambridge University Press, 2023), 17.

[36]"Religious Landscape Study," Pew Research Center, accessed September 9, 2023, www.pewresearch.org/religion/religious-landscape-study/party-affiliation/democrat-lean-dem; and Jeff Diamant, "Faith on the Hill 2023," Pew Research Center, January 3, 2023, www.pewresearch.org/religion/2023/01/03/faith-on-the-hill-2023.

[37]All three of these atheist thinkers are revered within American Christian nationalist circles.

[38]Djupe, Lewis, and Sokhey, *Full Armor of God*, 4.

[39]Lewis, *Four Loves*, 23.

[40]Lewis, *Four Loves*, 24.

[41]Richard J. Mouw, *How to Be a Patriotic Christian: Love of Country as Love of Neighbor* (Downers Grove, IL: InterVarsity Press, 2022), 14.

3. LEVIATHAN EMERGES

[1]Charlie Kirk, "Freedom Night in America: June 2021," YouTube, June 9, 2021, accessed November 14, 2023, www.youtube.com/watch?v=MjUO3dSLJao.

[2]Michael S. Heiser, *The Unseen Realm: Recovering the Supernatural Worldview of the Bible* (Bellingham, WA: Lexham Press, 2015), loc. 6530, Kindle.

[3]The one exception is found in Psalm 104:26, which shows that Yahweh tames Leviathan, who frolics in Yahweh's ordered creation.

[4]Lindsay Wilson, *Job*, Two Horizons Old Testament Commentary (Grand Rapids, MI: Eerdmans, 2015), 193.

[5]Richard Bauckham, *The Theology of the Book of Revelation* (Cambridge: Cambridge University Press, 2015), 89.

[6]Gregory, quoted in Manlio Simonetti and Marco Conti, eds., *Job*, Ancient Christian Commentary on Scripture (Downers Grove, IL: InterVarsity Press, 2006), 214.

[7]Mark A. Noll, *America's Book: The Rise and Decline of a Bible Civilization, 1794–1911* (New York: Oxford University Press, 2022).

[8]Mark A. Noll, *In the Beginning Was the Word: The Bible in American Public Life, 1492–1783* (New York: Oxford University Press, 2016).

[9]See Kaitlyn Schiess, *The Ballot and the Bible* (Grand Rapids, MI: Baker, 2023).

[10]*The Book of Eli*, directed by The Hughes Brothers (Los Angeles: Alcon Entertainment, 2010).

[11]Often attributed to sixteenth-century Italian philosopher Niccolò Machiavelli.

[12]Read the Doctrine of Discovery, 1493, at The Gilder Lehrman Institute of American History, accessed January 3, 2024, www.gilderlehrman.org/history -resources/spotlight-primary-source/doctrine-discovery-1493.

[13]See the work of Mark Noll, *In the Beginning Was the Word: The Bible in American Public Life, 1492–1783* (New York: Oxford University Press, 2016), and Abram C. Van Engen, *City on a Hill* (New Haven, CT: Yale University Press, 2020).

[14]Dave Verhaagen, *How White Evangelicals Think: The Psychology of White Conservative Christians* (Eugene, OR: Wipf & Stock, 2022), 63.

[15]While not specifically mentioned on the call, I believe this was referring to an event in January 2016 when Ryan and Ammon Bundy seized control of the Malheur National Wildlife Refuge headquarters in Oregon.

[16]Angela Denker, *Red State Christians: Understanding the Voters Who Elected Donald Trump* (Minneapolis: Fortress Press, 2019), loc. 153, Kindle.

[17]Luke Mogelson, *The Storm Is Here: An American Crucible* (New York: Penguin, 2022), loc. 3798, Kindle.

[18]Joe Carter, "The FAQs: Great Replacement Theory," The Gospel Coalition, May 19, 2022, www.thegospelcoalition.org/article/faqs-great-replacement -theory; Russell Moore, *Losing Our Religion: An Altar Call for Evangelical America* (New York: Penguin, 2023), 111.

[19]Public Religion Research Institute's 2021 survey notes that "Among those who believe God has granted America a special role in human history, 27% agree that violence might be necessary, compared to 12% among those who do not think God granted America a special role." "Ahead of Anniversary of 1/6 Insurrection, Republicans Remain Entangled in the Big Lie, Qanon, and Temptations Toward Political Violence," Public Religion Research Institute, January 4, 2022, www .prri.org/spotlight/anniversary-of-jan-6-insurrection.

[20]Angela Denker, *Red State Christians: Understanding the Voters Who Elected Donald Trump* (Minneapolis: Fortress Press, 2019) loc. 183, Kindle.

[21]Ryan Tafilowski, *"Dark, Depressing Riddle"* (Göttingen: Vandenhoeck & Ruprecht, 2019).

[22]Philip Yancey, *Reaching for the Invisible God: What Can We Expect to Find?* (Grand Rapids, MI: Zondervan, 2009), 66.

[23]This is not unique to American evangelicals, but Dave Verhaagen argues that there is a good amount of evidence from various studies showing conservatives (he included White evangelicals in this group) are more prone to fearfulness and anxiety. See Verhaagen, *How White Evangelicals Think*, 78.

[24]Alan Noble, "The Evangelical Persecution Complex," *Atlantic*, August 4, 2014, www .theatlantic.com/national/archive/2014/08/the-evangelical-persecution -complex/375506.

[25]David McRaney, *How Minds Change: The New Science of Belief, Opinion and Persuasion* (London: Oneworld, 2022), 172.

[26]Shawn Graves and Marlena Graves essay in Michael W. Austin and Gregory L. Bock, *QAnon, Chaos, and the Cross: Christianity and Conspiracy Theories* (Grand Rapids, MI: Eerdmans, 2023), 45.

[27]Samuel L. Perry and Cyrus Schleifer, "My Country, White or Wrong: Christian Nationalism, Race, and Blind Patriotism," *Ethnic and Racial Studies* 46, no. 7 (September 1, 2022): 1264, https://doi.org/10.1080/01419870.2022.2113420.

[28]Perry and Schleifer, "My Country, White or Wrong," 1264.

[29]James Baldwin, *Notes of a Native Son* (Boston: Beacon Press, 2012), 9.

[30]Katharine Hayhoe, *Saving Us: A Climate Scientist's Case for Hope and Healing in a Divided World* (New York: Simon and Schuster, 2021), 58.

4. LEVIATHAN EXPOSED

[1]Kristin Kobes Du Mez, *Jesus and John Wayne: How White Evangelicals Corrupted a Faith and Fractured a Nation* (Washington, DC: National Geographic Books, 2020), 4.

[2]Mark Charles and Soong-Chan Rah, *Unsettling Truths: The Ongoing, Dehumanizing Legacy of the Doctrine of Discovery* (Downers Grove, IL: InterVarsity Press, 2019); Peter Guardino, "'In the Name of Civilization and with a Bible in Their Hands': Religion and the 1846–48 Mexican-American War," *Mexican Studies*, October 1, 2014, 342-65.

[3]Paul A. Djupe, Andrew R. Lewis, and Anand E. Sokhey, *The Full Armor of God* (Cambridge: Cambridge University Press, 2023), 15; Russell Moore, "The Capital Attack Signaled a Post-Christian Church, Not Merely a Post-Christian Culture," *Christianity Today*, January 2022, www.christianitytoday.com/ct/2022 /january-web-only/january-6-attack-russell-moore-post-christian-church.html.

[4]Paul Miller, *The Religion of American Greatness: What's Wrong with Christian Nationalism* (Downers Grove, IL: InterVarsity Press, 2022), 198.

[5]C. S. Lewis, *The Four Loves* (New York: Houghton Mifflin Harcourt, 1991), 30.

[6]Mark A Noll, Nathan O. Hatch, and George M. Marsden, *The Search for Christian America* (Colorado Springs, CO: Helmers & Howard, 1989), 17.

[7]Paul G. Hiebert and R. Daniel Shaw, *Understanding Folk Religion: A Christian Response to Popular Beliefs and Practices* (Grand Rapids, MI: Baker, 2000), 378.

[8]Paul G. Hiebert, *Transforming Worldviews: An Anthropological Understanding of How People Change* (Grand Rapids, MI: Baker Academic, 2008), 9.

[9]David A. Ritchie and Yancey C. Arrington, *Why Do the Nations Rage? The Demonic Origin of Nationalism* (Eugene, OR: Wipf & Stock, 2022), 111.

[10]Michael J. Gorman, *Reading Revelation Responsibly: Uncivil Worship and Witness* (Eugene, OR: Cascade Books, 2011), 33.

[11]"Washington Revelations: Sites and Scriptures," Museum of the Bible, accessed August 19, 2023, www.museumofthebible.org/washington-revelations-sites -and-scriptures.

[12]Charlie Kirk, "TPUSA Faith Presents Freedom Square with Charlie Kirk," Turning Point USA, June 10, 2021, www.youtube.com/watch?v=gDaOS6YVR48.

[13]Paul D. Miller, *The Religion of American Greatness: What's Wrong with Christian Nationalism* (Downers Grove, IL: InterVarsity Press, 2022), 198.

[14]Jayson Georges, *The 3D Gospel: Ministry in Guilt, Shame, and Fear Cultures* (New York: Timē Press, 2017), loc. 214, Kindle.

[15]Miller, *Religion of American Greatness*, 6, 7.

[16]Angela Denker, *Red State Christians: Understanding the Voters Who Elected Donald Trump* (Minneapolis Fortress Press, 2019) loc. 214, Kindle.

[17]Karen Engle, "Biblical Literacy: What It Is and How to Reverse the Decline," Word by Word, May 31, 2022, www.logos.com/grow/biblical-literacy; "Americans Are Fond of the Bible, Don't Actually Read It," LifeWay Research, April 25, 2017, https://research.lifeway.com/2017/04/25/lifeway-research-americans-are-fond-of-the-bible-dont-actually-read-it.

[18]This Flashpoint promotion captures some of the popular claims: "2023: It's Time for Truth & Freedom," YouTube, accessed October 20, 2023, https://youtu.be/32Ae2q1tViI. See also Russell Moore, *Losing Our Religion: An Altar Call for Evangelical America* (New York: Penguin, 2023), 74.

[19]See Collin Hansen, *Young, Restless, Reformed* (Wheaton, IL: Crossway, 2008).

[20]David McRaney, *How Minds Change: The New Science of Belief, Opinion and Persuasion* (New York: Simon and Schuster, 2022), 165.

[21]McRaney, *How Minds Change*, 166.

[22]McRaney, *How Minds Change*, 169.

[23]I am indebted to my friends Jim Mullins and Chris Gonzalez for introducing me to the concept of political creatures.

[24]Both are forms of classical liberalism. See David T. Koyzis, *Political Visions and Illusions: A Survey & Christian Critique of Contemporary Ideologies* (Downers Grove, IL: InterVarsity Press, 2019).

[25]Brian Zahnd, "Evangelical Manifesto," *Brian Zahnd* (blog), June 8, 2008, https://brianzahnd.com/2008/06/evangelical-manifesto.

5. DISARMING LEVIATHAN

[1]Mark R. Glanville and Luke Glanville, *Refuge Reimagined: Biblical Kinship in Global Politics* (Downers Grove, IL: InterVarsity Press, 2021), 78.

[2]"14 Words," Anti-Defamation League, n.d., www.adl.org/resources/hate-symbol/14-words.

[3]There are a few versions of this concept, which was popularized by John Powell. See John Powell, *Why Am I Afraid to Tell You Who I Am?* (Chicago: Argus Communications, 1969).

[4]Joe Carter and John Coleman, *How to Argue Like Jesus: Learning Persuasion from History's Greatest Communicator* (Wheaton, IL: Crossway, 2008), 40.

[5]Carter and Coleman, *How to Argue like Jesus*, 23.

[6]Katharine Hayhoe, *Saving Us: A Climate Scientist's Case for Hope and Healing in a Divided World* (New York: Simon and Schuster, 2021), 15.

[7]Dave Verhaagen, *How White Evangelicals Think: The Psychology of White Conservative Christians* (Eugene, OR: Wipf & Stock, 2022), 142.

[8]David McRaney, *How Minds Change: The New Science of Belief, Opinion and Persuasion* (New York: Simon and Schuster, 2022), xviii.

[9]C. S. Lewis, *The Weight of Glory: And Other Addresses* (New York: HarperCollins, 1980), 46.

[10]Maria Cimperman, *Social Analysis for the 21st Century: How Faith Becomes Action* (Ossining, NY: Orbis, 2015), loc. 643, Kindle.

[11]Aleksandr I. Solzhenitsyn, *The Gulag Archipelago, Volume 1: An Experiment in Literary Investigation* (New York: Harper Perennial, 2020), loc. 2892, Kindle.

6. MEETING LEVIATHAN

[1]Chip Dodd, *The Voice of the Heart: A Call to Full Living*, 2nd ed. (Nashville: B&H, 2014), preface, loc. 65, Kindle.

[2]For more on discerning hurt and harm and setting healthy boundaries in your relationships, see Henry Cloud and John Townsend, "How to Discern Hurt from Harm in a Relationship," *Boundaries* (blog), September 19, 2022, www.boundaries books.com/blogs/boundaries-blog/how-to-discern-hurt-from-harm-in-a -relationship.

[3]Pamela Cooper-White, *The Psychology of Christian Nationalism: Why People Are Drawn in and How to Talk Across the Divide* (Minneapolis: Fortress Press, 2022), loc. 2305, Kindle.

7. ENGAGING LEVIATHAN

[1]For more on this posture, see Russell Moore, *Losing Our Religion: An Altar Call for Evangelical America* (New York: Penguin, 2023), 80.

[2]Lila Rose, Faith Pastors Conference 2022, Turning Point USA, San Diego, August 11, 2022, https://tpusafaith.com/summit22/.

[3]One example of this is Awaken Church's attempts to take over various government bodies in the San Diego area. Jakob McWinney, "The Group Seeking to Educate Conservatives to Influence Local Politics," *Voice of San Diego*, September 14, 2022, https://voiceofsandiego.org/2022/09/14/the-group-seeking-to -educate-conservatives-to-influence-local-politics.

[4]David Barton, Faith Pastors Conference 2022, Turning Point USA, San Diego, August 11, 2022, https://tpusafaith.com/summit22/.

[5]Rick Brown, Faith Pastors Conference 2022, Turning Point USA, San Diego, August 11, 2022, https://tpusafaith.com/summit22/.

[6]Sean Ellingson, Faith Pastors Conference 2022, Turning Point USA, San Diego, August 11, 2022, https://tpusafaith.com/summit22/.

[7]Hutz Hertzberg, Faith Pastors Conference 2022, Turning Point USA, San Diego, August 11, 2022, https://tpusafaith.com/summit22/.

[8]Raul Ries, Faith Pastors Conference 2022, Turning Point USA, San Diego, August 11, 2022, https://tpusafaith.com/summit22/.

[9]Rob McCoy, Faith Pastors Conference 2022, Turning Point USA, San Diego, August 11, 2022, https://tpusafaith.com/summit22/.

[10]Barton, Faith Pastors Conference 2022.

[11]Victor Marx, Faith Pastors Conference 2022, Turning Point USA, San Diego, August 11, 2022, https://tpusafaith.com/summit22/.

[12]McCoy, Faith Pastors Conference 2022.

[13]McCoy, Faith Pastors Conference 2022.

[14]Bob McEwan, Faith Pastors Conference 2022, Turning Point USA, San Diego, August 11, 2022, https://tpusafaith.com/summit22/.

[15]Brown, Faith Pastors Conference 2022.

[16]Michael O'Fallon, Faith Pastors Conference 2022, Turning Point USA, San Diego, August 11, 2022, https://tpusafaith.com/summit22/.

[17]Tim Alberta shares a similar story in *The Atlantic*. "The Politics of American Churches Are Changing," *The Atlantic*, June 2022, www.theatlantic.com/magazine /archive/2022/06/evangelical-church-pastors-political-radicalization/629631.

[18]Luke Barnett, "Jesus First," Faith Pastors Conference 2022, Turning Point USA, San Diego, August 11, 2022, https://tpusafaith.com/summit22/.

[19]Gary Hamrick, Faith Pastors Conference 2022, Turning Point USA, San Diego, August 11, 2022, https://tpusafaith.com/summit22/.

[20]Jurgen Matthesius, Faith Pastors Conference 2022, Turning Point USA, San Diego, August 11, 2022, https://tpusafaith.com/summit22/.

[21]McEwan, Faith Pastors Conference 2022.

[22]Barton, Faith Pastors Conference 2022.

[23]Jonathan Landry Cruse, "Why Corporate Worship Should Include Corporate Confession," The Gospel Coalition, January 26, 2021, www.thegospelcoalition .org/article/corporate-worship-confession; Peter C. Bower, *The Companion to the Book of Common Worship* (Louisville, KY: Presbyterian Publishing, 2003), 22.

[24]Public confession of systemic sins is a key part of the work of reconciliation. See Allan Aubrey, *Radical Reconciliation: Beyond Political Pietism and Christian Quietism* (Ossining, NY: Orbis, 2012).

[25]For a list of the 613 statutes in the Old Testament, see "613 Commandments," Wikipedia, accessed October 25, 2023, https://en.wikipedia.org/wiki/613 _commandments. For more on how these laws work in Scripture, check out the resources at the Bible Project, https://bibleproject.com/explore/video/law.

[26]Travis Mitchell, "Guns and Daily Life: Identity, Experiences, Activities and Involvement," Pew Research Center's Social & Demographic Trends Project, August 16, 2023, www.pewresearch.org/social-trends/2017/06/22/guns-and-daily-life-identity-experiences-activities-and-involvement.

[27]"Police, Military, and Firefighter Gifts," *No Greater Love Art*, accessed September 2, 2023, https://nogreaterloveart.com.

[28]For more on how the Scripture can shape our views on policing, see Esau McCaulley, *Reading While Black: African American Biblical Interpretation as an Exercise in Hope* (Downers Grove, IL: InterVarsity Press, 2020).

[29]When speaking about law enforcement it is important to note that there are a multitude of agencies, each with their own policies, histories, and protocols. Duren Banks, Joshua Hendrix, and Matthew Hickman, "National Sources of Law Enforcement Employment Data," US Department of Justice, revised October 4, 2016, https://bjs.ojp.gov/content/pub/pdf/nsleed.pdf.

[30]Michael Frost and Christiana Rice, *To Alter Your World: Partnering with God to Rebirth Our Communities* (Downers Grove, IL: InterVarsity Press, 2017), 132.

[31]"Charlie Kirk Speaks at 2020 CPAC," News 19 WLTX, February 27, 2020, www.youtube.com/watch?v=c-WiaPPxIHc.

[32]For more on the definitions of each category, see "Immigration Primer," *Evangelical Immigration Table*, accessed October 26, 2023, https://evangelicalimmigrationtable.com/resources/immigration-primer.

[33]For scriptural references and study guides see "Thinking Biblically About Immigrants and Immigration Reform," *Evangelical Immigration Table*, accessed October 26, 2023, https://evangelicalimmigrationtable.com/thinkingbiblically.

[34]Joe Carter, "Is the U.S. Constitution Divinely Inspired?," The Gospel Coalition, November 6, 2021, www.thegospelcoalition.org/article/constitution-divinely-inspired.

[35]Mark A. Noll, Nathan O. Hatch, and George M. Marsden, *The Search for Christian America* (Colorado Springs, CO: Helmers & Howard, 1989), 132.

[36]Transcripts of the original documents can be found at "America's Founding Documents," National Archives, accessed October 26, 2023, www.archives.gov/founding-docs.

[37]Luke Mogelson, *The Storm Is Here: An American Crucible* (New York: Penguin, 2022), loc. 419, Kindle. And yes, there are many who are not American Christian nationalists that use derisive, combative, and dehumanizing language. But that is for another book.

[38]"Republicans Draw from Apocalyptic Narratives to Inform 'Demoncrat' Conspiracy Theories," *Conversation*, accessed May 24, 2023, https://theconversation.com

/republicans-draw-from-apocalyptic-narratives-to-inform-demoncrat-conspiracy
-theories-170529.

[39]For example, see Lisa Sharon Harper and D. C. Innes, *Left, Right & Christ: Evangelical Faith in Politics* (Boise: Elevate, 2016); Justin Giboney, Michael Wear, and Chris Butler, *Compassion (&) Conviction: The AND Campaign's Guide to Faithful Civic Engagement* (Downers Grove, IL: InterVarsity Press, 2020).

[40]"Religion and Politics," Pew Research Center, accessed August 24, 2023, www
.pewresearch.org/religion/2021/02/16/religion-and-politics.

[41]Alan Noble, "The Evangelical Persecution Complex," *The Atlantic*, August 4, 2014, www.theatlantic.com/national/archive/2014/08/the-evangelical
-persecution-complex/375506.

[42]TPUSA hosts encourage their followers to share details about their local school board at "School Board Watchlist," www.schoolboardwatchlist.org.

[43]TPUSA takes a similar posture toward college and university professors via the "Professor Watchlist" website: www.professorwatchlist.org.

[44]Jeff Brumley, "Christian Nationalists Target Public Schools, Undermining Freedom of Religion, Webinar Guests Show," *Baptist News Global*, February 24, 2023, https://baptistnews.com/article/christian-nationalists-target-public
-schools-as-indoctrination-centers-webinar-guests-show.

[45]"Guidance on Constitutionally Protected Prayer and Religious Expression in Public Elementary and Secondary Schools," US Department of Education, May 15, 2023, www2.ed.gov/policy/gen/guid/religionandschools/prayer_guidance.html
?exp=1.

[46]The same goes for our understanding of schools throughout American history. For instance, there were many debates in the 1800s about the role of the Bible in public schools. See Warren Throckmorton, "The Cincinnati Bible Wars: When the KJV Was Removed from Public Schools," *Christian Post*, May 4, 2011, www
.christianpost.com/news/the-cincinnati-bible-wars-when-the-kjv-was
-removed-from-public-schools.html.